SOUTHWEST WISCONSIN LIBRARY SYSTEM

271.9   Kuhns, Elizabeth.
KUHNS
         The habit.

$23.95   10/21/2003

DATE		

WITHDRAWN

Prairie du Chien
Memorial Library
125 S. Wacouta
Prairie du Chien, WI 53821

D1064400

THE HABIT

THE HABIT

*A History of the Clothing
of Catholic Nuns*

Elizabeth Kuhns

DOUBLEDAY

New York   London   Toronto   Sydney   Auckland

Prairie du Chien
Memorial Library
125 S. Wacouta
Prairie du Chien, WI 53821

*14.16
Nov '03

PUBLISHED BY DOUBLEDAY
a division of Random House, Inc.

DOUBLEDAY and the portrayal of an anchor with a dolphin are registered
trademarks of Random House, Inc.

Book design by Donna Sinisgalli

Library of Congress Cataloging-in-Publication Data
Kuhns, Elizabeth.
The habit : a history of the clothing of Catholic nuns / by Elizabeth Kuhns.—
1st ed.
p. cm.
Includes bibliographical references and index.
1. Nuns—Clothing—History. 2. Monasticism and religious orders—Habit—
History. I. Title.

BX4223.K84 2003
271'.9—dc21
2003043522

ISBN 0-385-50588-4

Copyright © 2003 by Elizabeth Kuhns

All Rights Reserved

PRINTED IN THE UNITED STATES OF AMERICA

October 2003

First Edition

1 3 5 7 9 10 8 6 4 2

To my parents,

Bill and Kathy,

for teaching me the important things,

and for so much joy

Contents

Acknowledgments

I have been privileged to meet and work with extraordinary women religious. A few have become my close friends, but all are admired. These women have inspired me to grow in faith and in love, two things that they seem to exhibit in larger-than-life proportions each day in their work with the sick, the imprisoned, the marginalized, and the forgotten. Though my book focuses on a material artifact from their lives, I hope the reader will catch a glimpse of the remarkable courage and compassion that Catholic nuns have exhibited in every era of their history.

I have relied on contemporary women religious for much of my information, and I wish to thank those individuals who contributed specific resources, suggestions, insights, and explanations. Many sisters requested not to be specifically acknowledged, so I offer my thanks to those anonymous participants, as well as to the following: Sr. Maryalice Jacquinot, IHM; Sr. Mary Grace, Sisters of Charity of Our Lady, Mother of the Church; Sr. Beth Rindler, SFP; Sr. Theresa and Sr. Wilemina, Oblates of Mary, Queen of the Apostles; Mother Mary Patrick, AMM; Sr. Beth Murphy, OP; Sr. Miriam D. Ukeritis, CSJ; Sr. Marjorie Hamilton, RGS; Sr. Margaret Truran, OSB; Sr. Mary Loretta, Sisters of Life; Sr. Mary Elizabeth, Sisters of Life; Sr. Margaret Campbell, SNJM; Sr. Mary Anne Foley, CND, Ph.D.; Sr. Elizabeth McDonough, OP; Sr. Barbara Anne of CSMWR; Sr. Carole Mary

Capoun, CSSF; Sr. Barbara Garland, SC; Sr. Alma Mary Anderson, CSC, Sr. Agnes Gleeson, RSM; Sr. Winifred, SC; Sr. Andrew Persing, OSF; Sr. Marjorie Hamilton, RGS; Sr. Karen M. Kennelly, CSJ; Sr. Leonelle; Suzanne Delaney, IHM; Maria Hill, CSJ; Amy Levinthal; Reneta E. Webb, Ph.D., CAE; Arlene Ronollo, SSJ; Sr. Joan Miller, OSF; Sr. Therese Deveau, SMSM; and Sr. Gail Worcelo, Sisters of the Earth.

I wish to thank the following archivists and superiors of communities who provided me with materials and information from their private archival collections: Sr. Kathleen McNulty, IHM, Archivist, Congregation of Sisters, Servants of the Immaculate Heart of Mary; Ms. Loretta Zwolak Greene and Mr. Peter F. Schmid, CA, Sisters Providence Archives, Seattle, Washington; Sr. Genevieve Keusenkothen, Daughters of Charity of St. Vincent De Paul, West Central Province Archives, St. Louis, Missouri; Sr. Julie McGuire, CSC, Sisters of the Holy Cross; Ms. Patricia Jacobsen, Archives of the Little Company of Mary, Province of the Holy Spirit, Hurtsville, Australia; Ms. Cindy Swanson, Sisters of Bon Secours USA; Sr. Helen Streck, Adorers of the Blood of Christ, Wichita, Kansas; Sr. M. H. Sisters of the Good Shepherd, Province of Mid-North America, St. Louis, Missouri; Congregation of the Daughters of St. Francis of Assisi, American Province, Lacon, Illinois; Ms. Lisa Jacobson and Sr. Martha Bourne, Maryknoll Mission Archives, Maryknoll, New York; Monastery of St. Gertrude, Cottonwood, Idaho; Sr. Rita Rose Leding, Daughters of St. Mary of Providence, Chicago, Illinois; Mother M. Carmel, Sisters of the Presentation of the Blessed Virgin Mary, Watervliet, New York; Dr. Stephanie Morris; Sisters of the Blessed Sacrament; Sr. Donna Marie Kessler, Franciscan Sisters of Christian Charity; Sr. Mary Rose Chinor, Handmaids of the Sacred Heart of Jesus, Mary and Joseph; Sr. Antoinette Cedrone, Daughters of Mary Help of Christians-Salasian Sisters of St. John Bosco; Sr. Clare, The Community of Franciscan Sisters of the Renewal; Sr. Mary Laurence Hanley, Sisters of St.

Francis, Syracuse, New York; Phyllis Ann Lavalle, Sisters of the Most Holy Trinity, Euclid, Ohio; Sr. M. Nrimala, Missionaries of Charity, Calcutta, India; Sr. Carm Ternes, OSB, Monastery of St. Gertrude, Cottonwood, Idaho; Sr. M. Vaclava Ballon, Congregation of the Daughters of St. Francis of Assisi, American Province; Sr. M. Prostasia Hofstetter, Franciscan Sisters of Mary Immaculate, Amarillo, Texas; Sr. Mary Emmanuel, Daughters of Our Mother of Peace, Queen of Heavenly Solitude; and Sr. Mary de Paul, OP, Hawthorne Dominicans, Hawthorne, New York.

I would also like to thank Ken Cholewa; Fr. Juan Diego, OP; Dr. Desiree Koslin; Catherine Richardson; Brother Anthony of Adoramus House; the librarians at Marywood University, the University of Scranton, and the Albright Memorial Library, Scranton, Pennsylvania; members of the e-mail discussion groups "Sister-L" and "CTAC"; Sisters of Perpetual Indulgence; Fr. Thomas P. McCarthy; Dr. Cordelia Warr; Professor Giancarlo Rocca; Fr. Jay A. Finelli; Elizabeth Cardinal; Donna M. Steichen; Dr. Carol Coburn; Julia Ann O'Sullivan; Hugh Charles Martin; Lisa Jacobson; Dr. Dean Hoge; Fr. Anthony M. Patalano, OP; Dan Paulos, Fr. Augustine Thompson, OP, Ph.D.; Jim, Marilyn, and Michelle Shields; Joanne Francis; Amanda Powell; Maggie Hoerl, ACWR National Office; Maria Orzel, Diocese of Scranton; Dr. Margaret Susan Thompson; Dr. Asuncion Lavrin; Dr. Kathryn Burns; Mary Elizabeth Brown; Yvonne Goddard; Fr. Albert DiIanni; Susan Lloyd; Dr. Susan Michelman; Dr. Sarah Cline; Dr. Roger Finke; Dr. Patricia Ranft; Nicola DeGrandi; Fr. Michael Morris, OP, Ph.D.; Mary B. Dolan; Donna Sartor; Dr. Scott Hahn; Bridget Brewster; Carol Proietti, SSA; Dr. Marian Horvat; Duncan Maxwell Anderson; Barbara James; and Dr. Eric Plumer.

I would like to offer special thanks to Sr. Mary Catharine Perry, OP, and to Sr. Annmarie Sanders, IHM, for their extensive input and for connecting me to other resources; to Charles Coulombe for conceiving the idea for the book; to Dr. John P. Zmirak for his significant support; and to my agent, Christy Fletcher at Carlisle & Company, and Eric Major, Elizabeth Walter, Frances O'Connor, and Michelle Rapkin at Doubleday Religion for bringing the book to life.

Finally, I wish especially to acknowledge Martina Ciaruffoli Schuler for her expertise in clothing science and for contributing hundreds of hours of essential research for this book; Ray for his invaluable advice and editorial assistance; Rev. Calvin Goodwin, FSSP, for review of the manuscript; and my entire family for their help and encouragement, particularly Jeannette for providing French translation, and Eric for his incalculable contributions.

Introduction

$\mathcal{F}$or some, the Catholic nun's habit represents an outmoded Church and an obsolete way of life. Yet the distinctive black-and-white garb is a nostalgic image held dear by millions, serving as a universal representation of holiness—a mysterious and evocative cultural icon that has defined the Catholic sister for nearly two thousand years.

Because of the universality of the Catholic Church, the image of the nun is a familiar one, and whether Catholic sisters taught us in school or not, their lifestyles and attire fascinate us. When we speak of nuns, we tend to think of starched white linen headbands and wimples, long heavy woolen dresses, and flowing black veils. Although this form of attire is now more the exception than the rule, it continues to define our conception of the Catholic sister. Films and advertisements almost invariably use the habit to portray women religious, and the Church likewise uses the image because of the reaction it evokes from aspirants to convent life and potential donors alike. The habit lingers on because there is simply nothing as visually effective to take its place.

This book is dedicated to examining this extraordinary attire, which is richly complex and contains many unexpected paradoxes. For example, the habit's critics blame it for suppressing the individual, yet its proponents laud it for erasing class distinctions. Feminists see it as a symbol of patriarchial domination—a Christian analogue of the Moslem burqa—while traditionalists speak of the habit's ability to empower. Some blame it for separating the Church from the people, and still others credit it for creating fellowship and trust. It is hard to imagine how the same clothing, which epitomizes oppression and obsolescence to some sisters, can represent the ultimate beauty and dignity of the vocation to others.

The story begins at the dawn of Christianity, where the first consecrated women and earliest Church authorities shaped the habit's initial forms. Evolving from ascetic ideals, it traveled through medieval cloisters and knights' hospitals to the rugged frontier schools of the American West, taking on many shapes. Those worn by Benedictines and Dominicans, for example, were designed as monastic uniforms, specifically intended to distinguish women who had consecrated their lives to God. Other orders' habits, such as those that copied the "widow's weeds" or the working costumes of their times, came about from a desire to blend into society and among those whom the sisters served. The brown Carmelite habit has rarely been seen outside the monastery walls, while the white winged coronet of the Daughters of Charity became familiar even to non-Catholics as a model for the dramatic cap worn by Sally Field in the 1960s television series *The Flying Nun*. Examining the distinctions and similarities in the habits of different religious communities, as well as the unique symbolism and mystical rituals that accompany them, may help us to understand the complexities of this mysterious attire.

In the 1960s and 1970s, many religious sisters abandoned the habit, causing a universal sensation. It is a development laden with pain and bitterness, even among those who approved of the changes. Debate over the habit still rages today, and female religious orders are split down the middle on clothing issues. Two canonically approved membership organizations currently exist in the United States: the Leadership Conference of Women Religious (LCWR) and the Council of Major Superiors of Women Religious (CMSWR). The LCWR, the larger of the two, is made up of sisters who, for the most part, do not choose to wear a formal religious habit, while the newer CMSWR requires its member communities to do so.

Described by some as a "living cloister," many sisters see the habit as being at odds with their work in today's world. Others, however, believe strongly that it is an essential tool that opens doors. They also believe that by wearing the habit, they are following the wishes of Pope John Paul II, who as recently as 1996 in his apostolic exhortation *Vita Consecreta* expressly recommends male and female religious to dress in identifiable clothing, citing the Second Vatican Council's (1962–1965) insistence on the retention among religious of "identifiable garb." For these nuns, the habit is a wearable sacramental with a supernatural character that cannot be replicated in secular clothing.

Looking back, some link the disappearance of habits to the significant decline in the membership of female Catholic religious orders—a loss of approximately half of their members—over the past thirty years. Perhaps this explains why many new religious communities are incorporating the habit into their way of life.

Although raised as a Protestant, I grew up in the fundamentally Catholic city of Baltimore, where nuns were always present in my peripheral vision. From those glimpsed as I rode my bike past the brick convent at the end of my road to others passed in the school halls during rival athletic events, they were mysterious, black-robed figures in my girlhood landscape. It was not until years later, when I converted to Catholicism, that I began to understand the devotion and heroism of these women. With few exceptions, their lives of steadfast prayer and service, even in the face of extreme hardship and brutality, are models of the Christian ideal. As I began to form friendships with some of these serene, courageous women, I became curious about their clothing.

I found that myths and inaccuracies about the religious habit abound, and very little has been written about religious clothing and its history. In fact, the history of women religious has generally been ignored in literature until fairly recently, when feminist scholars and historians began to tackle this neglected topic. Regarding the habit specifically, no synthetic work exists in English to date. This book, then, opens the nuns' closet doors for the first time.

Given the huge scope of time covered, it can only serve as an introductory overview. I discuss a mere fraction of the thousands of orders that have existed within the Church, and I have not reported on religious habits from non-Catholic communities or secular institutes. Although I have used many important scholarly secondary sources, archival materials from religious communities, and Church documents, I have relied heavily on personal interviews for information. Many of the various opinions presented in this book are derived from conversations, letters, and e-mails from Catholic sisters all over the United States and abroad.

My book is a "popular" history, written from the viewpoint of someone working outside of religious and scholarly spheres. Although the text received review by clerical and religious persons, it remains a journalist's summary of an extremely complicated and far-reaching topic. I have provided notes at the end of the text to alert the reader to my sources, and to serve as a resource for locating further information. I have not always cited quotations and information available in general texts, or when extracted from my own interviews and correspondence. The bibliography contains a list of works used in the overall compilation of the book.

Religious life may be defined as the permanent mode of living of those who take three perpetual vows of poverty, chastity, and obedience within an institute approved by the Church. I use the terms "nun," "sister," "consecrated woman," and "religious" (the last is commonly used as a noun to refer to men and women who have taken the vows of religious life) interchangeably, although there are differences according to Church canonical law. I speak of convents, monasteries, and abbeys interchangeably as well, although there are juridical differences. Similarly, when I speak of a "community," it may mean "order," "congregation," "institute," or "association," although each has significant distinctions in canon law. Technically, the term "nun" refers to members of religious orders—who generally engage in "monastic" activities and who take "solemn" vows—while "sister" refers to members of religious "congregations," who work in "active" apostolates and who take "simple" vows. The title "Sister" is typically used for a female religious, and "Mother" is traditionally used to indicate the superior of a religious community. These terms, coupled with a religious name taken at the profession of vows, were in common use prior to Vatican II. Today many sisters prefer to identify themselves with their full birth names, followed by the initials of their order (often, but not always, from the Latin original), although both systems of nomenclature are in use and both appear in the text according to individual preference.

In describing the religious habit, some general terms are used which may not be familiar to the reader. "Habit" refers to the ensemble of clothing and accessories that make up religious dress. It can also mean specifically the robelike tunic or dress that is the main garment worn over the body. The "veil" is the long cloth worn on the top of the head, extending down the back. Some veils are designed to be pulled forward over the face, and other veils are designed as thin linings to wear beneath heavier veils. The veil is usually attached to a cap underneath, or "coif," which is a close-fitting cloth headpiece that conforms to the shape of the skull and often ties under the chin. A "wimple" or "guimpe" is the fabric piece that covers the neck and chest, and sometimes extends over the chin. A "bandeau" is the piece that stretches across the forehead, often attached at the ears behind the veil. A "scapular" is a long apronlike garment that is worn over the tunic and extends down both the front and back of the tunic. A "cincture" is a belt worn around the waist of the tunic, and a "Rosary" is a string of prayer beads and other objects often attached to the cincture and worn at the side. A "cappa," cape, or mantle refers to a cloak worn over the tunic.

Those who imagine that the topic of the habit is relevant in only religious spheres, separate from secular society, are utterly mistaken. As recently as the 1960s, for example, sisters who worked in the Ukraine were not allowed to wear any type of habit or religious insignia on pain of imprisonment; unfortunately, this remains the situation in China today. The communist government in the Ukraine at that time clearly understood the power of symbolic clothing. Although nuns receive their call from a supernatural source, and their mode of dress marks a distinct detachment from earthly things, their existence has always made an explicit impact on the world.

On the surface, it may seem frivolous to discuss the clothing—rather than the accomplishments—of women who built groundbreaking networks of schools and hospitals and who have generally been the most well-educated groups of females of their time. It might appear to trivialize the women who have continued to minister tirelessly to the spiritual and social needs of millions through almost two millennia. Yet it is important to remember that clothing is a uniquely human characteristic, a silent but powerful medium from which we can learn who we are and what we value. Clothing defines gender, status, beauty, and ideology, and it can be found in virtually every culture. It touches on human history, psychology, sociology, economics, aesthetics, technology, customs, laws, attitudes, and values.

The evolution of the shapes, colors, and fabrication of the habit distinctly reflects growth and changes in both the Church and secular society over many eras. Its symbols spoke to each age in which it existed, whether in the corridors of an eleventh-century German abbey or on a civil rights picket line in downtown Manhattan. Perhaps it is merely the persistence of the habit, however—regardless of its variety of manifestations—that may prove to be the most interesting. It is clothing that has provided a seamless link from the past to the present, and one that shows every sign of continuing into the future.

CHAPTER ONE

Enigma

A Catholic sister wearing religious garb can board a city bus and not be surprised if the bus driver places his hand over the fare box, insisting she ride free of charge. Respect for the habit remains universal—nun imposters who panhandle in city subways bank on wearing it to collect as much as $600 per day. It also can be an easy target for lampooning—consider the popular "Fighting Nun" puppet or the "Nunzilla" windup toy.

The nun's habit is one of the most widely known and recognizable religious symbols of our time, an icon deeply embedded in our cultural consciousness. Perhaps the habit has continued to fascinate us because of its unique blend of associations. As memoirist Mary Gordon recently wrote, "The image, the idea, of a nun brings together three powerful elements: God, women, and sex."[1]

At the same time that the habit serves to shroud the body and to mask the individual, it also dramatically announces its wearer to the world. The habit has the glamour of fashion while being antifashion; it is the antithesis of extravagance and sexual allure, yet it impresses and arouses. The sighting of a nun in habit remains for most of us a notable event, because what the habit proclaims is something so counterculture and so radical, we cannot help but to react with awe and reverence or with suspicion and disdain. From this clothing, we immediately recognize a woman who has decided to commit her life fully to

God, to renounce the possibility of bearing children, and to work within the boundaries of a community for some specific sacred purpose, frequently in neglected or controversial areas. She seems both less than female but greater than human—it was not unusual for schoolchildren of only a generation ago to believe that Sister had no hair, no legs, and no biological parents, for example.

Habit scholar Rebecca Sullivan notes that although the habit might seem like a static uniform, it has reacted to social and moral changes throughout history. It is a creative and imaginative clothing carefully constructed to impart meanings to its observers. It has also been used to instill unquestioning conformity and an identity that absorbs the self into a collective whole. Sometimes the habit replicated the clothing of the foundress of the community. It might have been designed by a bishop, or revealed in a mystical vision, or simply evolved from the peasant garb of the times. The habit embodied the mission of an order, joining together groups of women across the globe and across centuries in a common creative purpose.[2]

Today many people may not realize that sisters in North America who wear the habit are an exception rather than the norm. Most nuns say they have chosen to move to secular dress to serve their constituency better. But for some it has been a matter of personal autonomy, an emergence of the individual, and a reshaping of religious life. These sisters believe that secular clothing allows them to be approached as a "who" rather than a "what." Although public identifiability has long been a practice and law of the Church, they feel that the benefits gained from shedding the habit more than justify the change of attire. Some women religious have retained a symbolic ring or pendant, while others appear quite indistinguishable from laywomen, lipstick and jewelry included. But while it may seem that these sisters have become "invisible" on the streets and in parishes, they believe their actions are speaking louder than any physical symbols. And one nun notes, "They can still tell who we are. Our hair is too short, our skirts are too long, our shoes are too flat."[3]

It is this particular image to which many in the laity object. They do not want to see their cherished sisters as dumpy or unattractive— their plainness seems too close to the ordinary. Bonds formed with nuns in past generations were intensely visual and are not given up easily. Catholics cling to black-and-white memories of swishing skirts and tinkling rosary beads in the classroom and the kindly faces framed in fluted linen in hospital rooms. One contemporary Englishwoman reminisces, "I still have fond memories of the Faithful Companions of Jesus, at my old school, setting out in the sun and wearing floral sunbonnets over their black ones." She remembers the clothing long after she has lost connection to the person.

With their rapid disappearance, images of habit-clothed nuns have become more idealized and romanticized than ever. They are often used in the media and entertainment industries to grab attention and to sell products. Nuns in habit are irresistible subjects for journalists and advertisers, and this representation has become both piously saccharine and crassly kitsch at the same time. Cultural historian Jessica Matthews notes, "Items that can be found in specialty gift shops include nun squeaky toys, nun candles, nun puppets, nun lunchboxes, nun Halloween costumes, windup jumping nuns, strings of nun lights, postcards, comic books (*Warrior Nun Areala*), dolls, bookends, and coffee mugs that say 'It's a bad HABIT.'"[4] Additionally, the Internet teems with pornographic nun-related merchandise.

Most women religious—those who wear the habit and those who don't—are not happy about this phenomenon, which either perpetuates negative and inaccurate stereotypes or denigrates the sacred. The image of the cranky old nun in habit is one often utilized by cartoonists in the secular media, but its continued appearance in diocesan newspapers boggles sisters' minds. In September 2001 *The New World*, the newspaper of the Archdiocese of Chicago, ran an ad featuring a cartoon nun wielding a ruler. Many sisters protested, resulting in the subsequent printing of a halfhearted apology from the editor. On the other hand, some Catholic newspapers revere the habit so seriously that they refuse to feature photographs of sisters wearing secular clothing. This rankles women religious across the board.

These phenomena are not limited to religious publications. Bridget Brewster, director of communication and development for the Sisters of St. Joseph of Tipton, Indiana, tells of an experience with her local media:

> Following up a press release, the local newspaper sent a writer to do a story about the Sisters and particularly about St. Joseph Center and its use as a conference center and home for lay residents as well as Sisters. As is customary, a photographer was dispatched. I talked with the photographer at length.... "Please be respectful as you photograph individuals. It is my sincere hope that your photos will be an accurate and honest portrayal of the Sisters. These women are all about justice issues as well as their various ministries. Yes, they do gather for prayer daily as well as for Mass, however, that does not define them. Only two Sisters still wear a modified habit and veil and are not an accurate reflection of the Congregation. Please don't let me open the Sunday paper to find an 'icon of a nun in prayer.'"... The photographer understood and agreed. Well, as you have guessed, the large photo on the front page was one of the two Sisters in habit with a crucifix in the background! It is just too easy to convey a message with a veil and crucifix!... People simply do not want to let go of the image of the silly, innocent, naïve, pure, helpless nun that is seen through the habit.

The Catholic League for Religious and Civil Rights was founded in 1973 by the late Father Virgil C. Blum, SJ. The Catholic League defends the right of Catholics—lay and clergy alike—to participate in American public life without defamation or discrimination. The League believes that Catholic-bashing has become commonplace in

American society and regularly tracks negative images of nuns and the habit. For instance, in 1997 a coffeehouse in Nashville, Tennessee, sold a cinnamon bun designed to bear a likeness of Mother Teresa, called the "Nunbun," along with other products bearing her image. After protest from the League, the line was discontinued. In 1999 *Late Night with Conan O'Brien* kicked off the New Year with the host approaching an actress dressed as a Catholic nun and punching her in the face. That same year the League cited a *Saturday Night Live* episode featuring Rosie O'Donnell and Penny Marshall playing buffoon nuns in habit, with Marshall drinking liquor from a flask.

One of the most egregious objects of the League's protests is the Sisters of Perpetual Indulgence, a group of habit-dressed gay male political activists and performers. Established in the heart of San Francisco's Castro neighborhood in 1979, the male "sisters" commit as individuals to vows of community service and strive to "promulgate universal joy and expiate stigmatic guilt through habitual manifestation." League president William Donohue has petitioned the Internal Revenue Service to revoke the tax-exempt status of the Sisters of Perpetual Indulgence, explaining that: "If a group of anti-Semites were to dress as Shylock and mocked Jews, no one would excuse them because a small part of what they do is to contribute a pittance to selective charities."[5] The "sisters'" response to those who ask them why they "make fun of nuns" is that "We *are* nuns, who continue the essential work of traditional sisters in nontraditional ways."

The habit was an object of satire in secular art and literature even in medieval times. Today, however, no portrayal of nuns frustrates Catholic sisters more than those in the 1992 film *Sister Act*. In the film, Whoopi Goldberg plays a Reno singer on the run from her gangster boyfriend. She hides in an urban convent, disguised as a habit-clad nun. The juxtaposition of a lounge performer and a convent is a formula that propelled *Sister Act* into becoming one of the hundred top-grossing films in the United States of all time. It greatly offended many nuns, not so much because of Goldberg's character but because of the portrayal of the convent nuns, who were depicted as naïve and incompetent. It is a dated yet prevalent image that completely distorts what nuns really are like. Many women religious feel that *Sister Act* served to reinforce early stereotypes, such as those presented in *The Bells of St. Mary's* and *The Sound of Music*, perpetuating inaccurate perceptions of their lives formed in past generations. They believe these clichéd images of the habit have made them seem an anachronism precisely at a time when their contributions to society are so relevant.

Nonetheless, the habit sells. Belgian Sister Luc-Gabrielle, reluctantly stage-named Soeur Sourire (Sister Smile) by record promoters, had a blockbuster hit with "Dominique" in 1963. Clad in her white Dominican habit, the "Singing Nun," whose birth name was Jeanine Deckers, reached number one on the American charts, superseding even the Kingsmen's "Louie Louie." The image of a singing nun in habit was so appealing that in 1965 MGM made a musical film about her called *The Singing Nun*, starring Debbie Reynolds. Ironically, Sister Luc-Gabrielle later wrote a song in 1967 that included these lyrics: "To live in their midst consecrated, In shorts or dresses, blue jeans or pajamas."[6]

More than thirty years later, her wish has yet to come true. "The meaning of the habit shifts as the symbol is processed out of religious context and into a mass media image," says Sister Beth Murphy, OP, who has written on the topic and serves as communication coordinator for the Dominican Sisters of Springfield, Illinois. "Media images of priests and religious don't happen in a vacuum. They are complex social and cultural texts that carry diverse layers of meaning, subtly influenced by social and historical factors, among them, the experiences of real Catholic people." In 1965 nuns taught 30 to 40 percent of American Catholic schoolchildren.[7] Sister Beth theorizes that perhaps the proliferation of the habit image in the media is more about touching the hearts of this affluent and educated market segment and less about anti-Catholicism or misinformation. Baby-boomer Catholics want to see the image of the nun in habit, a distinct memory from their childhood. IBM recently cashed in with a commercially successful ad campaign featuring old-world Czechoslovakian nuns. In 2000 Jell-O ads depicted a sister in a traditional habit, licking her lips and staring longingly at a cup of pudding, with the tag line "I could go for something." Recently the noted purveyor of collectibles The Franklin Mint issued a commemorative plate showing nuns in black-and-white habits herding identically colored cattle through a field. The plate was titled "Holy Cow."[8]

In 1995 eighty women religious communications professionals formed the National Communicators Network for Women Religious (NCNWR) to address the image of sisters in the media. Other groups, such as Media Images of Religious Awareness (MIRA) and Sisters United News (SUN), also formed to try to change society's outdated and inaccurate perception of nuns. They believe that, beside the fact that few American sisters wear habits, the ideas of the unworldly, child-like nun incapable of managing her life, the tyrannical school nun, and the holier-than-thou nun all need reshaping.

Many sisters view Susan Sarandon's portrayal of Sister Helen Prejean in the film *Dead Man Walking* as a breakthrough, believing themselves accurately depicted in the media for the first time. Sister Helen relates that she had to explain to the film's director, Tim Robbins, that the nuns in her community, the Sisters of St. Joseph of Medaille, do not wear habits and were not originally required to do so by their seventeenth-century founder. She was adamant that her character be portrayed accurately, which included Sarandon's plain haircut and lack of makeup.[9] Many women religious were overjoyed with the film, honoring both Sister Helen and Susan Sarandon for their work. Similarly, MIRA chose to honor Ann Dowd for her nonhabited portrayal of Sister Maureen Peabody in the award-winning television series *Nothing Sacred.*

But what about nuns who do wear habits? Mother Teresa of Calcutta, art critic Sister Wendy Beckett, and cable television personality Mother Angelica are figures whose contemporary image has been fixed in the public mind partly through their clothing. These women command respect and admiration in religious and secular circles alike. Perhaps the habit has even furthered their causes. Mother Teresa's Missionaries of Charity are the fastest-growing order of women religious in the world, and Mother Angelica's Eternal Word Television Network (EWTN) has become the largest religious media network in the world, transmitting programming to more than 79 million homes in eighty-one countries. In these cases, the habit is an empowering, positive symbol, and it is quite hard to imagine any other clothing that can make this kind of a statement.

Although the habit is essentially humble clothing with a simple mission, many complexities are woven into the fabric. Like the vividly colored badges worn by seventeenth-century Mexican religious sisters, the clothing of Catholic nuns is not simply a black-and-white matter. The habit is a metaphor for the Catholic Church itself, subject to the human extremes of love and hatred.

CHAPTER TWO

Tradition

The nun's habit was once considered essential for establishing a new personal identity and sanctified lifestyle. During her clothing ceremony, an event familiar to many through its fairly accurate representation in the highly successful 1959 film *The Nun's Story*, the newly professed sister received her consecrated garb and new religious name in a ritual not unlike the christening of an infant. She then prostrated herself before the altar and allowed the presiding bishop to shroud her with a black funeral pall. Candles burned at each corner of her body while the choir sang the *"Dies irae"* (sequence from a requiem Mass), symbolically marking her death of self. From that point on, all references to her old life vanished. Transformed, she left her natural family to emerge reborn as a daughter of the Church.

Orders maintained traditions around the habit, sometimes for centuries. The ensemble was a rich, symbolic clothing prescribed in their various constitutions and revered by society. Each article had a specific meaning, relating the physical body to the spiritual realm. As a sister dressed, she meditated on the metaphorical messages of her clothing, regarding the habit as more of a devotional item than mere modest attire. The Little Company of Mary used the colors of their habit to relate these meanings, as stated in their constitution:

The black will remind the Sisters of their abandonment of the vanities of the world; the red will remind them of the Precious Blood, and of the Wounds of Jesus, and of the spirit of mortification; and the blue of the Immaculate Virgin, and of the purity of life which their vocation requires in habitual virtues.[1]

The habit of the Sisters Adorers of the Precious Blood had an even more elaborate set of symbolism. It is described in this way:

- Buttons on cape—Seven Last Words.
- Belt and sash—chastity and Precious Blood and cords used to bind Jesus at scourging.
- Veil—contempt for the world and reminds us of Veronica's veil.
- Tassels on shorter piece of Sash—Seven Bloody Sheddings.
- Tassels (lower)—Seven Sorrows of Mary.
- Chain bound link to link—our unending fealty to Christ.
- Heart—Source of the Divine Blood and the indissoluble union of Jesus and the Bride and reminds us of infinite love of God.
- Cross surmounting heart—our lot here is to bear the cross in order that the crown may be ours in heaven.
- Wimple and coronet—Crown of Thorns.
- Peaked coronet—direct thought upward.
- Habit—signifies poverty and reminds sisters of purple garment of mockery that Jesus wore.
- Cape—virginal modesty.
- Collar—yoke of religious life and reminds us that Jesus carried the sins of men on his shoulders. Three buttons signify the three nails.
- Frill—obedience and reminds us of the crown of thorns. The hairband signifies modesty of the eyes and reminds us of the cloth used to blindfold Jesus.

- Mantle—the hidden life of a religious and the hidden life of Jesus in the tabernacle.[2]

Special prayers were also commonly part of dressing rituals. The Congregation of Sisters, Servants of the Immaculate Heart of Mary, was founded in 1845 in Monroe, Michigan, by Father Louis Florent Gillet and Mother Theresa Maxis. The sisters were originally called the Sisters of Providence and wore a black habit, but in 1847, when the Church decreed Mary Immaculate as patroness of the United States, Mother Theresa and the sisters petitioned to change the title of the community to a name that would honor the Blessed Mother. They replaced their black habit with a blue one, a color symbolic of the Blessed Mother, and the professed sisters adopted a gold ring engraved with the words *Ego te sponsabo* (I will wed thee). After dressing in the blue tunic, a sister prayed "May the Most Holy Virgin clothe me with her holy habit." Donning the blue scapular was accompanied by "May the most Holy Virgin clothe me in her virtues." After the black cincture came "Gird me, O Lord with a cincture of purity, and destroy in me all seeds of lust, and let constancy and chastity ever reign within me." Upon putting on the Crucifix, each sister prayed, "Let me die for love of thee, Oh Lord, who didst expire on the cross for the love of me," and finally, after putting on the veil, "Place, Oh Lord, upon my head the helmet of salvation, and defend me against the assault of the enemy."[3]

The Franciscan Sisters of Mary Immaculate had no set prayers outlined in their rule or constitutions while dressing but customarily prayed, "Lord Jesus Christ, through your suffering in having the white garment placed on you as a mockery, grant me the grace not to sully the innocence of my soul today." When undressing, they recited, "Lord Jesus Christ, through the pain you did feel when stripped of your garments, forgive me all the sins which I have committed today through the three faculties of my soul: memory, understanding and free will, against the purity of body and soul."[4]

The Development of a Habit

When a new community formed, there was much to consider in creating a habit. Men were usually involved in the decision making, but some participated in the design phase as well. The Sisters of St. Francis of Philadelphia received their habit from Bishop John Neuman, who invested them with a simple black dress. The Franciscan Missionaries of St. Joseph noted that their nineteenth-century bishop tried on their headdress in order to make suggestions on improvements in the style. In 1904 the Holy See ruled that the Sisters of Loretto add a white lining to their veil to break up the monotony of the all-black habit, which church officials believed would detract from attracting new recruits. The superior of this community responded to the order stating that they had an abundance of candidates and did not appreciate the clerical encroachment into matters of their dress. However, some priests provided excellent and welcome advice, since they were free to move about from town to town and could relate information about fabrication and designs seen among other orders.[5]

The Maryknoll Sisters were founded in 1912 at Maryknoll, New York, for foreign mission work. In fact, they were the first congregation of Catholic religious women in the United States to be founded for this purpose. In 1920 they were canonically approved as the Foreign Mission Sisters of St. Dominic, and when they later became a Pontifical Institute (community approved by Rome) in 1954, their name was changed to Maryknoll Sisters of St. Dominic.

Their foundress, Mother Joseph, was born Mary Josephine Rogers in Boston, on October 27, 1882. While at Smith College, Mary Josephine had organized a Mission Study Club for the Catholic students at Smith with the encouragement of the Reverend James A. Walsh, then director of the Society for the Propagation of the Faith in Boston. She began assisting Father Walsh in the work of mission education, and in 1911 Father Walsh and Father Thomas Frederick Price began a seminary to train American young men for the foreign missions, called The Catholic Foreign Mission Society of America (more commonly known as Maryknoll Fathers and Brothers).

Father Walsh chose Mary Josephine to lead the group of "secretaries," as the women were called prior to their becoming recognized as sisters, and she was eventually elected mother general of the order. The first Maryknoll sisters dressed in secular clothes in the style of the times. In 1912 the community obtained permission to adopt a uniform dress. Mother Mary Joseph designed it with the subsequent approval of Father Walsh. The sisters recorded the following in their 1912 newsletter, under the item "How to Dress":

> Mr. and Mrs. Michael Maginnis and Miss Tomoney of New York visisted the seminary and the two latter had dinner with us. We had much discussion the night before, as to how we could possibly entertain two fashionable dressmakers in our garments of ancient make. But when the time came we quite forgot how we looked; and Mary Joseph even rose to the point of asking for a sample of Mr. Maginnis' gray suit, which she thought would be excellent for the long cloaks that are faintly visible on our horizon....
>
> Father Lane also paid us a short visit. He tried to solve our millinery problem by suggesting the widow-like bonnet worn by Protestant deaconesses; but we were almost as horrified at this as [at] Father Walsh's suggestion of sailor hats. The best scheme so far is the one suggested by Mrs. Maginnis and Miss Tomoney: toques made of the same material as the cloaks.

The Maryknoll habit incorporated a uniform gray felt hat and warm gray coat. The hats had round brims and round crowns, trimmed with a band of gray velvet. Before the community chose a regular head-dress, the sisters wore their hair parted in the middle and rolled in the back. In 1913 the newsletter, now called the "Maryknoll Distaff," made these comments about the development of a headdress:

That night Mary Joseph brought up the question of headgear. They had realized the need of some kind of head covering ever since they have had the Blessed Sacrament in the house, for they were continually searching for their veils or missing a visit in the chapel because they had no head covering with them. Mary Augustine suggested gray veils to be worn constantly; but most of them preferred Mary Joseph's idea of some sort of Dutch bonnet made of white linen, like their collars and cuffs. Their efforts at making paper patterns were not very successful; but they agreed that the headdress, when approved, should be given to the postulants on arrival as their part of the uniform and the part most easy to provide.

Sarah fashioned a cap out of a piece of linen; Mary Joseph combed her hair back in the approved style—or lack of it—and put on the cap while the others amused themselves with the effect. That "game of caps" continued the following night, Eve of Memorial Day. Father suggested a three-cornered arrangement symbolic of the Trinity and the command to teach all nations, baptizing them in the name of the father, and of the Son, and of the Holy Spirit. Anna worked out something on this line for Mary Joseph to model. Then the model appeared before Father, who thought the cap too suggestive of a religious order for the Teresians' [an early name for early Maryknolls] stage of development. He advised getting something less conspicuous by trying the same shape in gray or making the white shape smaller. Will the Community Song be "Put on your old gray bonnet?"

By June 1914 the "secretaries" wore gray cotton gingham uniforms with full plaited skirt, a tight belt, and plain shirtwaist attached. Over the belt they wore a gray cincture with the Chi Rho monogram (the first two letter letters of the Greek word for "Christ") embroidered in blue. A short cape was worn over the shirt and was attached with gray smoke pearl buttons. It incorporated a white, turned-down, stiffly starched collar that opened in front, along with white starched cuffs fastened with gray buttons at the wrist.

During 1915 the sisters added long gray capes. In 1916 the archbishop enrolled fifteen women as Dominican tertiaries. These sisters received a small white scapular to be worn under the uniform. The community continued to wear the gray cape and hat for traveling, and used a black chiffon veil held in place with a plastic band when attending chapel.

As late as 1918 there was still no definite headdress, and by 1920 the community had experimented for some time with headgear. Postulants at this time were assigned a dark blue poplin dress with a short cape, without buttons or a cincture. Sisters who took private vows, before the community was recognized by Rome, wore the silver Chi Rho rings. In 1920 the habit reached its nearly final form. It was fashioned from gray cotton with long white scapular, over which was a gray scapular with cincture that threaded from front to back. The cape was cut on the bias and came to a point in the front. The sisters also adopted the Miraculous Medal as part of the habit. In 1929 they began making the habit from woolen fabric, and the long white scapular was discontinued in 1931, with a small white one worn underneath instead.

In September 1942 the fabric of the postulant headdress changed to voile for everyday and celinese for feast days, with a white starched band worn across the head in front. The habit in its final form was made of gray tropical-weight serge with the scapular made from the same fabric. The veil was draped over a frame of buckram and wire, forming a point over the face. The cincture was of the same material as the tunic and was embroidered in blue silk with the Chi Rho, the blue color honoring the Virgin Mary. Their mantle or cloak was black, and not worn in the tropics. The habit included a fifteen-decade Rosary with four extra beads for prayers to be said for their "absent sisters." The Rosary was made from Job's tears beads strung on black fishnet twine by each sister before she received the habit. Their ring, symbolizing faith, was a signet style with the Chi Rho letters in a raised design and was worn on the third finger of the left hand. Sisters assigned to missionary work received a "Missioner's Crucifix" in black and silver worn on a gray cord. Over their tunic was a cape of the same fabric finished at the top with an added white collar.[6]

The Clothing Ceremony

The habit was so intrinsically linked to the order and the nun's life that it was nearly impossible to separate one from the other. By adopting new clothing, the sister publicly became part of a new spiritual family, and the reception of the habit was the very dramatic passageway from one way of life into another. During postulancy, candidates wore a modified version of the habit or modest street clothes, such as a white blouse and black skirt. The ceremony of becoming a novice and taking the holy habit marked a change in status as well as complete alteration of identity. The following is an excerpt from the ritual used by Dominicans from 1930 until the 1960s to bestow the habit, from the *Ceremonial for the Nuns and Sisters of the Order of Friars Preacher:*

> At the hour appointed, the Mass being finished (or the Vespers) if before the Clothing it could be celebrated, the Priest who presides at the ceremony of the Clothing (vested in Cappa and white stole, if a Priest of the Order, otherwise in

surplice and stole, or, where it is the custom, vested in Cappa and Stole) goes and sits near the grill, and to the postulant or postulants to be clothed—prostrate in the Choir of Nuns—speaks as follows in the vernacular: *What do you ask?* And she (or they) replies: *God's mercy and yours.*

Then the President gives her (or them) the signal to arise, while he expounds the nature of the religious vocation and the austerities of the Order. At the end of the instruction, the President says to her: *Do you wish to receive the holy Habit and to observe the Constitutions of the Nuns of the Sacred Order of Preachers?*

And she replies: *Yes, Reverend Father, this I wish and desire by the grace of God.* The President then subjoins: *May the Lord who has begun this bring it to perfection.* And the community replies: *Amen.*

The President then says: *Exuat te Dominus.*

Then the President, kneeling, intones to note (or merely recites, if the Postulant is to receive the Habit of Lay-Sister) the hymn: *Veni, Creator . . .* which the Choir continues in alternate verses.

At the end of the first verse of the hymn, the President rises and stands at the foot of the Altar or near the grill, while the Prioress (assisted by the Mistress of Novices, and other Sisters if necessary) gives the religious habit to the Postulant within the choir itself or in some suitable place adjacent to the choir. The Postulant, however, before receiving the white veil, approaches the communion-window in the grill, and there the President cuts off some of her hair with a scissors.

At the end of the hymn, the choir sings: *Kyrie eleison, Christe Eleison, Kyrie Eleison,* and the President says: *Pater noster . . .* which all recite in secret.

The President sings (or recites) the versicles and the prayers.

After the Prayer: *Dilectissimae Sorores . . .* the President gives to the newly clothed Novice, kneeling at the communion-window of the grill, the Crucifix (and Rosary) saying: *Accipe, Soror carissima* . . .

He then says: *Dominus custodiat* . . .

The hymn: *Jesu, corona Virginum* . . . is then sung by the choir, in the following or in any other tone. [music is provided]

During the singing of the hymn, the President offers the Novice two crowns: one made of roses and the other of thorns, saying: *Behold, my dear child, two crowns: one precious, the other of thorns, choose that with which you wish to be crowned.*

The Novice choosing the thorns, says: *I choose the crown of thorns.*

The President then says: *Accipe, Soror carissima* . . .

Then the President blesses with holy water the Novice wearing the crown of thorns.

After this, the President gives to the Novice a religious name, saying: *In the world, you were called N.N.* . . . , *in the Order, your name shall be Sister N.N.*

To the aspirant, on the reception of the Habit, may be given a new name, without, however, renouncing that received in baptism. After the Clothing the Nuns shall always prefix to their religious name the word Sister, and likewise when referring to others.

The hymn *Te Deum* . . . is then sung by the choir, while the Novice receives the kiss of peace from the Sisters.

The President, having sung the prayer after the *Te Deaum,* concludes the ceremony with the versicle: *Adjutorium nostrum* . . .

The Mistress of Novices shall register in the *Book of Receptions to the Habit* the verbal process of the clothing, inserting the:

1) Baptismal and family name of the Novice;

2) Religious name given her on reception to the Habit;

3) Baptismal and family name of the parents of the Novice;

4) Place and date of birth and of the baptism of the Novice;

5) Day and hour of beginning her novitiate.

The year of the novitiate began the same day as the reception of the habit and ended on the close of the same date of the same month of the following year. The final profession could then be made any time following the day of the anniversary of the "Clothing."[7]

Sposae Christi

By the middle of the tenth century, the clothing ceremony for many nuns represented an elaborate secular marriage ceremony, including a High Mass and special episcopal blessing of the veil, with the sister being given away by her father or male guardian. She became the Bride of Christ, symbolized with a ring and crown.[8] The Benedictine profession ceremony placed a silver ring on the nun's finger after which she replied, "I am espoused to Him Whom angels serve; Whose beauty sun and moon behold with wonder."

Espoused to the Heavenly Bridegroom, she dressed in a white gown and veil, wore orange blossoms in her hair—a bridal custom that originated in ancient Rome—and carried flowers. Although the color white was used for Greek and Hebrew brides, it fell out of fashion in the West until late in the Romantic period. Roman brides wore red until the Renaissance, and red is still the bridal color in India. The Church in the east did not place as much of a focus on the bridal imagery, and there was always less of a distinction between male and female monastic garb. For example, some Eastern nuns took a hooded head covering.

The gathering afterward—sometimes the last time a nun would be able to visit freely with her family—often featured a wedding cake. The sister assumed a new name. In some orders she chose it herself, while in others it was assigned to her. The occasion had all the festivity of a secular wedding or debutante ball. Many women carefully styled and curled their hair; others enjoyed various worldly luxuries for the last time.[9]

Since the earliest days of the Church, nuns were called the spouses of Christ—St. Cyprian describes a virgin who had broken her religious vows as an "adulteress." Although the imagery has all but vanished from most modern profession ceremonies, even as late as the 1960s, it was a common event. Some orders provided the wedding dresses for the women; others requested them from the postulant's family, removing the white lace later on for use in making vestments.[10] All of the former garments were left behind, including feminine lingerie, which was exchanged for basic white cotton pieces.

In addition to a dowry, a postulant's family often was required to provide a trousseau. In the 1970s the Sisters of the Holy Family in Louisiana required a dowry and personal supplies that would last the nun for three years. The Sisters of the Holy Cross suggested this list of trousseau items in 1960:

> 4 black shirt waists (not silk)—Koolcloth, poplins, or broadcloth
>
> 3 black underskirts—Sateen, poplin, or broadcloth
>
> 2 gingham underskirts
>
> 2 gingham aprons with bibs
>
> 3 outing flannel gowns, if you wish
>
> 3 muslin nightgowns with long sleeves
>
> 1 black or dark blue kimono
>
> 1 black or dark blue woolen bathrobe
>
> 8 changes of knit underclothing—not silk
>
> Vests with long sleeves (for winter and summer)
>
> 6 brassieres—plain
>
> 2 girdles—not satin
>
> 2 sanitary belts
>
> 4 hand towels (Turkish or linen)

4 bath towels

4 wash cloths

12 handkerchiefs (men's size)

1 black Sleeveless knitted sweater button front

1 black double shawl (woolen or cashmere not knitted)

1 pair black silk or lisle gloves

8 pair black cotton or lisle hose

1 pair black bedroom slippers (soft soles and heels)

1 pair black oxfords—rubber heels 1½ inch heel. Flat heels are not permitted. (1 Pr. At time of entrances two other pairs during Postulancy and Novitiate.) Shoes should be large enough to allow for exercise.

1 pair rubbers (not toe rubbers)

1 pair galoshes

2 tooth brushes, tooth paste

1 hair brush

2 combs—bobby pins, shower caps

Nail scissors and file

Unscented powdered Mennen's or Johnson's

Non-scented soap

Hand lotion

Deodorant—dress shields

Stationery—plain white

Pen and pencil

Loose-leaf binder

Paper for binder 8½ × 11

Sewing box—black and white darning cotton and thread, thimble, needles, darning egg, measuring tape, scissors, straight and safety pins

Shoe polish kit

Clothes brush

1 mirror

6 linen table napkins

1 table service (viz.: knife, fork, tea and soupspoons)

1 white spread—for single bed

1 double bed size blanket—woolen

4 pillow cases—large size

4 sheets for single bed

25 yards of bleached muslin

2½ yards of batiste, for veils

15 yards of black serge, 56 in.

1 umbrella

1 black suitcase

1 trunk

Daily Missal (suggested St. Andrews)

Following of Christ, Holy Bible, *Liber Usualis* (J. Fisher & Bros. NY
Pub.), Dictionary (Webster's Collegiate), Black rosary and
case

Novitiate expenses $200

Reception fee $10

Collars $2

Teeth checked and report signed by dentist

Change shell rimmed glasses for rimless glasses

The following articles should *not* be brought to the Novitiate:

Electric clock

Picture albums

Scrap books

Year books

Razors

Flash light

Zippers on underskirts

Face powder—dusting powder

Cold cream[11]

Class Structure

Although the habit was designed in part to erase social distinctions among women religious, the distinctions between "lay" and "choir" sisters remained in place until around 1967, when the Holy See ruled that the class of lay sister, also called *conversae*, was to be abolished. This provision for a working, servant class of nun, typically less educated than "full-fledged" sisters, had a long history. The lay sisters assumed the household duties of the order, performing most of the manual tasks such as cooking, cleaning, and farming. Although choir sisters also participated in these labors, more often they busied themselves with finer modes of work, such as needlework and calligraphy. Because lay sisters were not schooled in Latin, they recited "Hail Mary" and "Our Father" prayers while the choir nuns chanted the Divine Office, or they perhaps prayed the Little Office of the Blessed Virgin Mary in the vernacular. Often the lay sisters would take on the more rigorous post-midnight rosary duty, performed while the choir sisters were asleep. They had their own common room and their own mistress, who was a choir nun, and were banned from voting on matters affecting the community. In many orders, the lay sisters' entire habit was different, usually a less elaborate version of that of the choir sisters. Dominican lay sisters wore a white veil until they were presented with a black one in 1967. It is possible that some very traditional orders retain some kind of unspoken choir and lay distinction in their ranks.

There were also nuns designated as "externs" who communicated with the outside world, living outside of enclosure. They were considered a slightly higher class than lay sisters, because they would have had to have been educated enough to conduct business affairs for the choir nuns. The need for this kind of distinction disappeared with the advent of active orders, beginning in some cases in the seventeenth century, when most sisters were free to move about in the world as they deemed necessary.

The habit also helped to distinguish another type of social division. For example, there were distinctions across communities, and some congregations were regarded as more prestigious than others. Historian Margaret Thompson notes that when heiress Katherine Drexel of Philadelphia, for example, wished to become a nun in 1880, she expressed interest in joining the Franciscans. However, her spiritual director pointed her to a different order, stating of the Franciscans, "They are not ladies. There is not one of them that would have a much stronger claim to be considered such than your maid Johanna. . . . For a lady of your antecedents, position, and habits, to be able to pass her whole life in the most intimate daily and hourly intercourse with women of the peasant class, would require a fortitude that is vouchsafed to few indeed."

The Sisters of Mercy sought to develop at least one "select" school as part of their organization, in order to attract candidates from wealthier backgrounds. The Adrian Dominicans made a reference to being "blue-lined" (barred) from opening an academy at their motherhouse, a reference to the blue habits of the Servants of the Immaculate Heart of Mary, who were favored by the bishop. In the African American community, one Holy Family sister remembers being steered to the "higher-class" Oblate Sisters of Providence by relatives.[12]

The Habit in Daily Life

The sister in charge of discipline at the Sacred Heart schools had the title of "surveillant." Every aspect of a nun's daily life was closely monitored to foster extreme self-restraint. A sister had to request permission to make a phone call, to visit a doctor, and to procure personal items. Books and newspapers were often forbidden, and incoming and outgoing correspondence was censored. A sister had to ask for permission to obtain something as trivial as a piece of thread. Bells guided daily movements, and faults were recorded in little books. Some of these practices may seem cruel or prisonlike, but it would not be accurate to assume that all sisters were unhappy with the regulations, which were a part of the way of life they had freely chosen. However, many of these directives probably hung on because they were part of a "Rule" (set of church-approved guidelines for the order) that had been created decades or centuries earlier. Another explanation for the adherence to these regulations is that when communities were in periods of reform, they often looked to the past for renewal, incorporating old practices as a means of strengthening unity of purpose.

Many regulations regarding modesty related directly to the body. To keep "custody of the eyes" meant that sisters must normally direct their eyes downward and ensure that they did not move from side to side. It was illicit in some orders to look a man directly in the eye for any reason or to gaze at any worldly things for too long, such as items in a shop window. Voices were kept low, and emotion was not to be displayed. Even food was taken in silence, with special hand signals used to communicate, such as a knife-drawn circle on the tablecloth to indicate "pass the salt." If something fell on the floor and disturbed the silence, the offending sister would kiss the item in reparation.[13]

Walking was to be accomplished in a calm, demure manner—hurrying was discouraged. Sisters were taught a specific set of movements, with hands tucked out of sight underneath their scapular. The habit assisted in creating the sort of soft, sweeping, movements that were desired. Some cloistered nuns' veils featured a fold-down flap that allowed the sisters to pull a veil over their face when faced with an "outsider." One sister recalls: "Getting through a profession ceremony with candles, books, ceremonies etc., with the lowered veil was not easy. Nor was escorting plumbers, electricians, etc., through the house and pointing out what was wrong."

Fabrication

By the middle of the twentieth century, the habit had become so different from the dress of secular society that many modern sisters recall that it felt like putting on a theatrical costume. For others, its uniqueness was its appeal, as most communities made their own habits inhouse, fabricated according to precise measurements and patterns. Because each ensemble so represented its respective community, any deviations would have been unthinkable. Even when an article of the habit might have become archaic or obsolete, it continued to be worn and created from the original direction using original materials if possible. For example, directions for making a day cap of the Sisters of the Holy Cross read:

> The day cap consists of three parts, the headpiece, the crownpiece and the border. The headpiece is as wide as to fit the head and in length to correspond to the length of face. The outer edge is hemmed $\frac{2}{3}''$ wide. The crownpiece is left plain on each side for three inches and then it is gathered with one row of stitching to fit the headpiece. The lower part is hemmed. The border is of Victoria Lawn, from 3 to $3\frac{1}{2}$ yards (9 to $10\frac{1}{2}$ feet) long. It is $4\frac{1}{4}''$ wide including the hem which is $\frac{5}{8}''$ wide. It is gathered with two rows of stitching to fit the headpiece. After gathered border has been stitched to the outer edge of the cap it is hemmed with tape. The tape is inserted around the whole cap and drawn through the hem of the crown piece and tied.[14]

In addition to typical materials, headpieces often featured complicated wiring and other unconventional materials to give their shape. Some communities used the plastic from Clorox bottles as a stiffening form in their foreheadbands. Many veils and coifs included wire framing, such as those of the School Sisters of Notre Dame, whose headdress featured a squared-off top. In the 1950s and 1960s, some textile companies produced a fabric for nuns that bonded linen to a kind of early plastic called celluloid. It did not require starching and washed and wore very well. However, it was discovered to be highly flammable, so the material was discontinued. Most habits were made of wool serge, an almost indestructible fabric. Later on some habits were made of polyester, rayon, and cotton blends.

Beyond a distinctive headdress or scapular, each community also had its own distinct Rosary, often attached to the belt or cincture and worn at the side. Franciscans almost always used a seven-decade Rosary, while the Dominicans used a fifteen-decade Rosary. The Franciscans commonly used brown beads and the Dominicans black oval beads, while some communities included the Miraculous Medal in their Rosary design. In the same manner, communities also had a unique crucifix. Some were embossed or engraved with symbols, letters, or mottoes; others held relics, such as a minute bit of splinter from the True Cross or other small holy relics.

In addition to the precise instructions and patterns that existed in the official documents of a community, some orders created miniature models of the habit. Nun dolls were popular from the mid-seventeenth to the end of the eighteenth century. They were created either as a collection of figures or as individual pieces and were not playthings. They might have been inspired by French fashion dolls that were sent to other European countries so that clothing designs could be copied or from figures fashioned of the nativity scene. Until the 1920s, dolls were used so the habit could be reproduced among orders separated by distance. A collection in the Victoria and Albert Museum in London includes a figure of the pope and secular canons and canonesses. Many communities have them in their private collections.

From the beginning of the seventeenth century, there was an effort to reform the dress of women religious, as individuals had begun adding furs, ribbons, and other ornaments illicitly. Nun dolls were used to codify habits, and there are early records of Carmelite dolls being sent to new foundations in Mexico, for example. Others were sent to a Carmelite convent in Knock, Ireland, in the 1920s for just this reason. The Rule for the Paris Ursulines stated in 1705: "So that nothing in the habit is changed there must be kept in a triple-locked coffer or archives the 'Form' [doll] of a choir sister and a lay sister dressed in the same material and style that are used at the present time, as laid down in Article 180 of the Constitutions." The canonesses of St. Augustine at Hassocks, near Brighton, England, originating from a community established in Bruges in penal times, have a nineteenth-century doll dressed with great accuracy, down to the unusual knitted stockings and the pocketbook of improving maxims that each sister compiled for her own use.

Nun dolls were also treasured by private families. Once a daughter left her family, her parents might not have been able to afford to travel to see her again or to have a portrait painted. A doll was an inexpensive, portable way of showing a nun's family how she was dressed, serving as a treasured personal reminder. In the archives of St. Mary's Abbey, Colwich, England, there is a letter from Sister Placide Brindle describing her clothing in a convent in Paris in 1768. In a postscript she says, "Betty Simeon has sent mother a little nun which paid us a visit before it set out and I suppose you have seen the little one Sister Agens sent her father, then you may see which dress you like the best." These dolls continued to be popular in France for First Communion gifts. St. Thérèse of Lisieux's family had this custom, for example. Pauline Martin, Thérèse's sister, owned a paper doll dressed as a Visitation nun. The Lisieux Carmel sent young Thérèse a doll dressed as a Carmelite, which might have inspired her to choose this order over others.[15]

Maintenance of the Holy Habit

Habits were often designed to minimize their need for replacement. The Sisters of Mercy used special "dress sleeves" for example, that would button onto the habit bodice for Mass and prayers, replacing the normal "work" sleeves. Dominican nuns wore (and some still do) coveralls when performing manual labor—a tunic of brown or blue fabric. The Dominican habit was so simply designed that it could be turned and worn with either side facing front. Many communities taught sisters to elevate slightly their habits or walk in a certain way to avoid damaging their garments from repeated movements. The sister in charge of clothing often was required to seek permission for a new habit to be blessed by a priest before it could be distributed.

Since earliest times, it was the practice in religious communities to keep laundering to a bare minimum. A stress on simplicity in lifestyle meant that modern washing machines, even after they became commonplace in secular society, were seldom used by religious orders, if at all. As late as the 1970s some Carmelite monasteries washed their thick bedsheets only once a year. All maintenance procedures were specifically outlined in the rule and could not be altered. Dry cleaning was too worldly a practice for most communities, so woolen habits were generally only spot cleaned and washed thoroughly perhaps once or twice a year, with only undergarments being changed daily. Some orders prohibited a full immersion of the habit and showered it with soap and water instead; others permitted washing in baking soda only. After a hot day, a woolen habit could become very unpleasant smelling, and as standards of hygiene improved some congregations chose to switch to using fabrics that were more easily laundered.

Founded in Algeria in the 1930s, the Little Sisters of Jesus chose to wear denim habits, which they considered the practical cloth of the working class. The bodice of their dress featured a red felt heart and a brown felt cross. Sisters wore a leather belt, to which was attached a simple wooden rosary, held fast with a practical snap clip. Their veil was a blue peasant-style kerchief tied at the neck behind the head, and they wore sandals.[16]

In most orders, each sister was assigned a number with which to mark her clothes, and maintenance was accomplished by sisters selected for the task, sometimes overseen by a "vestiarian." The 1855 Holy

Cross Rule book states: "231. Each sister in the Society has a special number, whatever is marked with it will be given to them until worn out, so that each can answer for her own effects." Because old laundry methods were preferred, many sisters recall having skinned hands or bloody fingers after a day of washing with harsh chemicals and rudimentary devices.[17] Many items required elaborate starching and pressing. Some orders handled things very simply—pressing a veil flat under a mattress, for example. Other habits required hot and cold starching. This process involved boiling water and powdered starch together and dipping the cloth items into the mixture. Then the item was placed on wax paper and into a freezer. When needed, it was removed, thawed, and ironed with a hot iron. This stiffening method was used for collars, guimpes, and bandeaus.

Before Vatican II, the Servants of the Mother of God wore a heavy black serge habit with large oversleeves, a blue scapular, a blinkered headdress, and heavy black shoes for nursing. But in general, nuns' nursing habits were white and changed daily to ensure proper sanitation. They were designed with tighter-fitting sleeves and slimmer skirts for the same reason. The work required to maintain habits was daunting—one wimple could take ninety minutes to starch and iron, for example. In 1923 the vicaress of the Sisters Adorers of the Precious Blood wrote the mother general a response to her petition to wear a less complicated "flat" cap as opposed to a fluted frilled cap:

> Reverend Mother General, the growing discontent among the Sisters, arising from the uncertainty of receiving a simpler and less burdensome headdress, causes me great anxiety and grieves me greatly. I so well realize that their duties in church and in school are so multiplied and their short vacation period must largely be spent in arduous and exhausting summer school work. The very little time that is daily left to them—time that should really be given to rest and relaxation—must be laboriously spent in laying, sewing and especially in *fluting* their frills.[18]

Not only were these complicated headpieces time-consuming to maintain, they often caused the wearer physical harm. One sister from an American congregation recalls:

> The fluted cap, once adjusted, fit pretty tightly to the head. (I ended up needing a skin transplant on the edge of one ear because of the rubbing of the fluted cap over the day cap.) If you recall the band over the forehead, that and the day cap under it provided a fairly good base for all. The veil was pinned to the fluted cap, behind the cupcake part, and unless we were caught in a very stiff wind, or unless our veil was jerked really hard, the headgear was pretty stable.

Many nuns developed deep ridges over their eyebrows where the headband had rested for so many years or developed migraine headaches from headgear that was too tight. Others believed that the elaborate headdresses made them seem like an anachronism and an object of ridicule. A superior of the Sisters Adorers of the Precious Blood wrote:

> Already, our Sisters have been subjected to the most humiliating ridicule for the round plate-effect of the flat cap. They have been called picture frames, sunflowers, electric light globes, etc. The Sisters are furthermore convinced that the still more unattractive appearance of the flat cap would induce our American girls to enter other Orders, whose members wear a head dress that has a more religious appearance.[19]

Nuns were not supposed to be concerned with appearance, however. Many communities forbade sisters from looking in a mirror, an action considered a sign of vanity. Most nuns cut their hair very short, or even shaved their heads entirely, to keep hair covered by the coif more easily. Sometimes sisters were issued wigs when they had to go out of the convents on business and when their superior determined they should not dress in habits, such as for classes at a university. When nuns changed habits after Vatican II, many had hair in terrible condition from years of poor circulation and friction beneath layers of fabric.

Small Changes

Once the habit became established, it rarely changed in design or form. However, some orders did make updates for the sake of comfort, safety, availability of materials, and maintenance. The headdress of the Dominican Sisters of Edmunds went through several changes from 1847 to 1960. In 1846 the guimpe was starched into tiny pleats. In 1902 the guimpe took on the appearance of ruffles, perhaps because the missionary sisters did not have the means to make the tiny pleats. The veil at this time was pliable. In 1905 the guimpe was completely flat and was worn this way only for a short time. In 1915 the guimpe was starched into various flat shapes. The veil was also stiffened. By 1942 the veil had gotten much stiffer, and the guimpe again became pliable. In 1952 the stiff veil was voted out and replaced by a white-lined soft veil with a cardboard top.[20] The Missionary Sisters of the Holy Ghost's constitution was written to allow for the reevaluation of the habit every five years.

Scapulars were shortened for work that involved machinery. A community of St. Augustine Canonesses included culottes in their missionary habits because they had to ride mules in the Philippine mountains and could not ride sidesaddle, a previous practice that had caused the death of one of their members.[21] In another example, a Sister of Providence recalls, "When permission came from the Alaskan Sisters to wear nice warm and hooded parkas, that was a great boon, especially appreciated by those keeping yard duty! Another great innovation."[22]

Yet these kinds of changes remained the exception. Even when reasons for maintaining current customs and designs were no longer clear, orders were hesitant to deviate from original models. When superiors initiated modifications, women religious often rallied against them. Sisters were so loyal to their habit that few would so much as consider adding an extra stitch to a fold. Preservation of the past was sacrosanct in most orders—something like a proposal to use disposable sanitary napkins, rather than old-fashioned washable cotton cloths, elicited suspicion. Sometimes it was simply a matter of sheer numbers. The Sisters of Charity did not choose to update their starched white coronette until very late in their history, because doing so required the outfitting of up to 45,000 sisters with new headgear, an expensive and time-consuming proposition.

So sisters continued on into the modern age, wearing stifling wool in summer and sometimes freezing outside in winter because nothing more than a shawl would fit around their elaborate uniforms. Skirts caught in car and bus doors, and their flowing sleeves tangled in machinery. Their vision was impaired for driving by blinkered headwear. Thus, by the 1950s, some leaders thought the habit was in need of change. But they were without a willing following—so deeply engrained in the psyche of the nuns and so important in attracting new recruits, the habit was not to be tampered with. Sisters thought that if the habit altered in even the minutest of details, their lives would change irrevocably as a result. This led to an explosive situation in the 1960s that would result in dramatic and far-reaching consequences. But how did clothing attain this dramatic level of importance in sisters' lives? Perhaps going back to its beginning and examining the evolution of this extraordinary garb will help explain its mystique.

CHAPTER THREE

Holiness

𝒯he earliest Christians who wished to consecrate their lives to God sometimes donned sacred garb without ceremony or clerical oversight, privately transforming their outward appearance to reflect their spiritual commitment. The holy habit itself, however, is actually older than any formal rites of avowal, which were not universally instituted until late in the third century. Adopting this special clothing self-imposed the essence of the vocation—a promise of poverty, chastity, and obedience—on the wearer. During these formative years of Christianity, the act of changing clothes *was* the act of religious profession by those who aspired to holiness.

The apostle St. Paul wrote to the early Church at Galatians, "There does not exist among you Jew or Greek, slave or free, male or female, all are one in Christ Jesus." At a time when most of society was subject to a ruling, upper-class patriarchy, this was a radical statement with profound implications. Its revolutionary leveling of sexual and social groupings may offer some insight into the origins of monastic clothing, garb which has always been virtually the same for all holy men and women. Through the ages, the consecrated dress code has varied little from the plain wide-sleeved tunic, belt, scapular, cloak, and simple footwear, the only difference being in the style of headgear.[1] This lowly costume was designed from its beginnings to contrast sharply with the clothing of the privileged classes, to which many early Christians belonged—some even went as far as to don their own servants' garments. This novel austerity no doubt appealed to the early transformed religious who wished to make a bold statement about their new life in Christ, giving physical evidence of their singular calling.

The Dawn of Christianity

Typical secular dress for women of the ancient biblical world ranged from the Greek *chilton*—a voluminous and finely pleated draped covering—to the Spartan split skirt that bared the thighs and permitted greater freedom of movement. The *chilton* was fashioned from rectangles of cloth held together by pins or brooches and kept in place by a belt or cord around the waist. The Doric *chilton* was made of wool, and its Ionic counterpart was fashioned from linen, the latter being more flexible and therefore able to incorporate a greater number of folds. Wealthy citizens wore richly hued fabrics, often with decorative borders. The poor generally used white or natural-colored fabric, which they sometimes dyed a reddish brown, even though civic law forbade them to do so. Over the *chilton*, Greek women wore a long, cloaklike garment called the *peplos*. Those who could afford them wore sandals— some elaborately decorated. A surviving pair of courtesan's sandals featured soles studded with nails designed to imprint the words "follow me" into the ground as she walked.

The ancients of the civilized world considered draped clothing superior to the loosely tailored, stitched clothing of barbarians. Patrician Roman women wore a long, draped inner tunic, initially made of wool and then of linen, cotton, or silk. Similar to the Greek *chilton*, this garment was also worn by men under the toga. Favorite fabric colors were red, yellow, and blue, often with lavish embroidery and gold fringe. A sleeved garment called the *stola* covered the tunic, and a ruffle on the *stola* may have distinguished married women from prostitutes. Matrons often used a shawl-like *palla* outdoors along with elaborately decorated slippers and a veil. Sometimes veils were pulled down over the face.

Prostitutes wore a togalike gauzy covering and were assigned their identifiable costume by statute. At one time, Roman law also required women in this profession to have blond hair, either natural or bleached. Cosmetics, perfumes, hair dyes, scarves, caps, ribbons, intricate hair-dressing, scrupulous bathing, and the meticulous removal of body hair were as common among Greek and Roman housewives as among prostitutes. As lavishly as they could afford, all classes of women wore gold, silver, and jeweled bracelets, armbands, tiaras, earrings, anklets, toe and finger rings, and hair accessories. Female ancients incorporated into their costumes fans, handbags, and handkerchiefs, which were used as status symbols.

The women of antiquity lavished great attention on their appearance, and dress was such a symbol of wealth that the Roman Oppian Laws of the first century B.C. were enacted to regulate displays of ostentation. Clothing was highly political at this time, regulated by ordinances and strong social customs. Each social rank had detailed regulations outlined regarding the shape, color, and textiles of their clothing, down to the size of stitching and number of knots used in fabrication. But as with sumptuary legislation of any epoch, the regulations often were ignored, and both men and women defied authority to make a fashion statement or simply to revel in luxuries forbidden them.

Respectable Jewish women, on the other hand, wore more modest clothing usually made of wool or linen. As with Greeks and Romans, Jewish matrons usually were veiled in public. Hebrew clothing was based on the principle that more was better. Slaves, for example, were required to wear shorter garments that revealed their legs. In Jewish culture, proper clothing was essential to a well-ordered society with right relationships, and it was equated with strength and power. Although Greeks viewed nakedness as an aesthetic and philosophical ideal, it was forbidden in Jewish society and symbolized shame and loss of honor. God made Adam and Eve coverings of skins and clothed them Himself (Gen. 3:21), for example. Old Testament priestly garments linked the wearer to the transcendence of God and were made only from pure fabrics; the mixing of wool and linen fibers was not allowed (Lev. 19:19). The last chapter in Proverbs describes the biblical ideal of the "valiant" Jewish woman in terms of her connection with textiles:

> She hath put out her hand to strong things, and her fingers have taken hold of the spindle. She hath opened her hand to the needy, and stretched out her hands to the poor. She shall not fear for her house in the cold of snow: for all her domestics are clothed in double garments. She hath made for herself clothing of tapestry: fine linen, and purple is her covering . . .[2]

Making clothes was considered a suitable home occupation for wives, queens, and even goddesses, although professionals often carried out weaving, dyeing, and finishing. Fabrics were not always indigenous. Romans were importing luxurious silk cloth from China as early as the first century A.D. The first female Christian converts would have likely continued to wear the dress of their ethnic heritage. They expected Christ to return in their lifetimes and saw no need to distinguish themselves through dress. During times of persecution it could have been dangerous for the converts to wear distinctive garb.[3] Yet it became important for some Christians to dress themselves as representatives of the new Church in a conspicuous, recognizable fashion, so observers would know of their allegiance. For those who chose the special religious calling of virginity, the early religious habit offered both a visual symbol of consecration and practical physical protection. For women in particular, the rough, undraped clothing served to hide the contours of their bodies, acting as a sort of armor against sexual advances. It also concealed instruments of self-mortification, such as branches of thorns, shirts or girdles of haircloth, belts of nails, and other devices worn next to the skin that the wearer wished to remain unseen by others.

It is hard to imagine what first caused individuals to desire such severe apparel and how specific holy clothing became so necessary to Catholic religious life. Indeed, the appeal of Christianity itself seems mysterious, when we consider the unspeakable tortures and brutal deaths that many suffered in the Roman Colosseum in order to hold fast to their faith. Yet text from Sacred Scripture and writings of the Church Fathers and first great monastic leaders, who treated the subject of Christian dress with great importance, offer precise explanations for the beginnings of many Christian traditions of religious dress and appearance. Some of the foremost early female martyrs demonstrated deep commitment to the concept of holy and modest clothing. Throughout the centuries, the attraction of the habit has remained strong enough to cause masses of believers to defy families, friends, and governments in order to wear it, beginning with the contemporaries of Christ and continuing even to this day.

Imitation of Christ

Early Christian baptism involved shedding one's old clothes and putting on new white robes, representative of Christ Himself, as explained by St. Paul: "For as many of you as have been baptized in Christ, [you] have put on Christ" (Gal. 3:27). The new robe was called by Church Fathers the "clothing of immortality." When Christ revealed his divine glory to some of the apostles, his garments became "white as snow" (Matt. 17:2).

Because He was God as well as man, Jesus Christ embodied human perfection, and as a sinless being, He served as the model for all Christians. His mother, the Blessed Virgin Mary, was also conceived without original sin, providing a second model for believers. Therefore, the individual who adopted Christian religious life was called to the task of emulating these two persons, both pure and immaculate, in the hope of an ultimate reward of eternal life with God. This emulation included a detachment from all earthly things. Christ told his followers in the Gospel of St. John, "My kingdom is not of this world" (John 18:36) and taught the figurative lesson in the Gospel of St. Luke: "If any man come to me and hate not his father, and mother, and wife, and children, and brethren, and sisters, yea and his own life also, he cannot be my disciple" (Luke 14:26). Jesus stressed throughout His ministry the necessity of making a choice between the things of this world and the glory of the next. Religious life began then as a separation.

Christ lived a life of poverty, chastity, and obedience, teaching that nothing impure would enter the gates of heaven. St. Thomas Aquinas later explained that holiness was the act of making all our actions subservient to God, and Christian followers who devoted their lives to religious contemplation subjected themselves completely to divine authority, giving themselves over to God in an attempt to abandon an imperfect or inferior existence. From the beginning, religious dress had a sacred nature and served to sanctify the body, setting the religious person apart from the world. Its derivation from Sacred Tradition, and therefore from divine origins rather than human ideas, drove the habit's acceptance and perhaps explains its longevity. The strictly voluntary nature of the religious vocation is also an important distinction. Those who donned the first habits to follow Christ did so of their own free will.

The First Nuns

The earliest images of nuns are found in missals and other liturgical books. Yet groups of virgins and widows participated in eremitic and communal asceticism long before any of these drawings were made. Nuns date to the very inception of the Church, when women consecrated themselves to God and religion for its own sake—for instance, orders of widows are mentioned in the Acts of the Apostles and in the Epistles of St. Paul. Virgins referred to themselves as Brides of Christ and set themselves apart from society, initially living with their families but later forming their own communities. Jesus' own friends, Martha and Mary of Bethany, sisters of Lazarus whom Christ raised from the dead, would go on to serve as the archetypes of all female religious orders. Through her service to others, Martha represented the active, or apostolic, side of religious vocation while Mary demonstrated the contemplative nature of the lifestyle—according to tradition, she eventually became a hermit. The first Christian women were Jewish, but Romans and Greeks quickly embraced the new religion as well.

When the teachings of Christ were implicitly followed, the lives of females improved dramatically. One of the most significant societal changes instituted by Christianity was the restoration of the lifelong monogamous marriage, which Christ elevated to the status of a sacrament, making it a religious calling rather than mere civic union. St. Paul instructed in his first letter to the Corinthians, "but yet neither is the man without the woman, nor the woman without the man, in the Lord," reinforcing Christ's attitudes toward the dignity and mutual dependence of both sexes, each created in the image of God. From the earliest times, Christianity sought to free women from demeaning pagan practices and unjust constraints. This was especially notable at a time when Imperial Rome was busy restoring the old ancestral codes that rewarded citizens for marrying and bearing at least three children and sanctioned those couples who did not meet their reproductive quota. Because marriage was held in such low esteem, polygamy and divorce were common and male and female prostitution abounded. Spartan women enjoyed slightly more status and were given the opportunity to control property when men were at war. Rarely seen in public, Athenian women held very low status and married very young. Greek girls received little or no education, and all women, regardless of age, were legally classified as children.

Against the social norm, women often accompanied Christ in His travels throughout His ministry. The evangelist St. Luke lists Mary Magdalene, Joanna (a married woman), Susanna, and "many others who ministered unto him of their substance" as followers. Jesus Christ broke with Jewish tradition by speaking to women in public and eating meals with them. He even allowed a woman with a gynecological disorder to be healed by touching the hem of his garment at a time when men and women could not touch each other outside of marriage and when women with discharges from menstruation or childbirth were considered symbolically "unclean."

Sociologist Rodney Stark suggests that Christian women outnumbered Christian men in the first century, reasoning that Christianity prohibited female infanticide—a practice that was legal in the pagan Greco-Roman world—and abortion (a major cause of death in adult women due to crude methods). Ancient and modern historians also agree that conversions to the new religion were more prevalent among women than men. This phenomenon holds true with many other religions, and can be seen in nineteenth-century records of Shakers, Christian Scientists, and Spiritualists. In the first five centuries of Christianity, the Church also attracted a remarkable number of highborn women. This aided the spread of the religion significantly, as these women could use their influence on high-status pagan husbands to convert, release Christian prisoners, or protect the Church. For example, Marcia, the concubine of Emperor Commodus, prevailed on him to free Callistus, a future pope, from the salt mines of Sardinia.

Stark also notes that, in his epistles, St. Paul frequently extended warm greetings to prominent females in the Church and praised their work. Because the first churches were communities that met at the houses of Christian followers, the hospitality and domestic expertise of women played a significant part in establishing Christianity's initial foothold in the world. Widows who gained control of their own wealth and property patronized the early Church generously, supporting its outreach into foreign lands and financing many of its first buildings and monuments.[4]

The new religion also gave women unique opportunities to teach, study, and write. Christ recognized a woman's intellect and treated her with uncommon dignity—in his parables, he highlighted male and female characters and scenarios equitably. Novelist and Christian writer Dorothy L. Sayers insightfully summarized Christ's revolutionary attitudes toward women in her book *Are Women Human?*

> Perhaps it is no wonder that the women were first at the Cradle and last at the Cross. They had never known a man like this Man—there never has been such another. A prophet and teacher who never nagged at them, never flattered or coaxed or patronized . . . who took their questions and arguments seriously; who never mapped out their sphere for them, never urged them to be feminine or jeered at them for being female; who had no axe to grind and no uneasy male dignity to defend; who took them as he found them and was completely unselfconscious.[5]

Christ's vision of womanhood was certainly far different from the widely held Aristotelian conception of women as incomplete or "mutilated" men. Female Christians made a meaningful contribution to the ministry of the early Church by supporting Jesus, witnessing and testifying to the resurrection, carrying out mission work, prophesying, and ministering to other women. In order for the Church to spread as rapidly as it did, it was perhaps necessary for women to abide by some of the ethnic and social norms of gender roles in place at the time. The Church does not accept as authentic any accounts of women serving as legitimate priests or bishops in the primitive Church, and great debate rages as to the exact nature of their early ecclesiastical roles. However, several distinct and important female groups within the Church were widely recognized by the apostles and the first Christian leaders.

This elevation of woman also centered on Mary, the mother of

Jesus. Considered the purest virgin as well as the model mother, she exemplified both perfect tenderness and tremendous strength. The Catholic Church has displayed a constant affirmation of this sublime position of Mary—in Christian art, the Virgin has been the highest representation of the nobility of womanhood. As the second Eve, Mary lifted the curse of the first Eve, who had been guilty of original sin. One tradition holds that after Christ's death, Mary became the first nun. In medieval art, however, she was never depicted in the black veil of the professed nun but often portrayed in blue, a color that symbolized purity at the time.[6] Some believed that Mary lived in community with other virgins, perhaps organizing the first religious order herself.

Virgins, Widows, and Deaconesses

The Greek and Roman worship of virgin goddesses glorified females independent of men, but this esteem did not carry over to mortal females. Women's roles were defined strictly through marriage and motherhood—no acceptable position existed for the single, free woman. Roman law specifically required a woman to be bound in marriage or registered as a prostitute. One exception was the famous group of Vestal Virgins, a cultic community of women who tended the Roman Fires of State. A Vestal was chosen by lot to serve between the ages of six and ten, bestowing great honor to her family. Thereafter, she lived completely apart from her family with her sister Vestals, wearing a long, sleeveless white gown, girdled at the waist and draped with a loose robe. Her hair was cut short at her investiture and decorated with ribbons. She wore on her head the headband of a Roman matron with a veil fastened underneath her chin. The Vestal pledged her virginity for thirty years under the penalty of being buried alive at the Campus Sceleratus (Field of Crime).[7]

Isis was a chaste Egyptian goddess whose Roman followers practiced a sort of asceticism with shorn hair and modestly cut linen garments, but Christian virgins were the first to set themselves apart in a total lifestyle completely distinguished from ordinary norms. They believed their promise of complete chastity and renunciation of riches connected them to God in an exceptional manner. Christ spoke of the righteousness of self-imposed virginity and viewed it as something more laudable than marriage; this was a radically new idea. It granted women autonomous significance, and the virgin who forsook marriage gained preeminence over the married woman. Virgins were often described by their peers as "manly," because masculinity was the equivalent of the highest virtue, and taking the vow of virginity required great courage. Virginity was considered a full-fledged movement by the end of the first century. A significant number of the early Christian martyrs were virgins who would not renounce their vows even under extreme familial or political pressure.

In A.D. 177 Cecilia, a maiden from a rich and distinguished Roman family, convinced her fiancé to allow her to preserve her virginity. But officials eventually executed Cecilia, her husband, and her brother-in-law for their refusal to renounce Christianity. Friends clothed her body in rich silk and gold, including a veil, for burial, and her body remained incorrupt for centuries. This phenomenon was fully documented when her body was exhumed in 1599. When the examiners searched the body for relics, they found that she wore a hairshirt underneath her burial clothes. St. Agnes, a virgin martyr of the third or fourth century, died by the sword to preserve her purity. According to legend, Agnes was stripped of her clothes by her ruthless persecutors and exposed in a brothel; her hair miraculously gathered around her virginal body as a protective covering until she received a white robe from heaven.

Taking vows of virginity, men and women of any social strata were able to travel and work together as chaste partners for the first time. Women also could choose to live together in groups, relying on each other for help and support rather than on fathers and husbands. In the times of persecution, consecrated women and widows lived within the existing Christian communities. Later they moved to the desert or outside urban areas. Paul's Acts of the Apostles speaks of virgins who prophesied (Acts 21:8–9).

As the concept of the virginal lifestyle became accepted, so did the role of the nun. Although St. Anthony (b. 251) is considered the father of monasticism, documents reveal that he placed his sister in a "house of virgins" before he left for Egypt to establish the first ascetic community of men. The Church defines the purpose of virginity as the preservation of perfect chastity in one who abstains from sexual pleasure. It teaches that a woman retains her virginity after bodily violation if it was committed against her will. Catholic tradition holds that the bodily integrity of the Blessed Virgin Mary was preserved even in the act of giving birth to Jesus.

Virginity was considered a noble triumph over base appetites—it created a special likeness to Christ, Himself a virgin. Chastity was one way of renouncing the ties of this world, and a chaste life was often compared to a "life like that of the angels." St. Paul taught that the state of virginity was to be preferred to the state of marriage: "Therefore, both he that giveth his virgin in marriage, doth well; and he that giveth her not, doth better." The Council of Trent later pronounced an anathema against believing otherwise. Reminiscent of the Vestals of Rome, Christian virgins underwent their own clothing ceremony when they made a profession of their intended vocation. The bishop presided, and the consecration of virgins and their clothes became a sacramental rite. Church Father St. Jerome (ca. 342–420) spoke of the *mutatio vestium* (ritual change of clothes) of a young girl vowed to virginity, which entailed her being "clothed in a dark-colored tunic, wrapped in somber cloaks and having her linen garments taken away."[8] Virgins at first continued to live at home with their parents and siblings, but at the end of the third century they gathered together in community houses. They were a special class in the Church and received

Holy Communion before the laity. In the ancient Litany of the Saints prayer, they are distinguished along with widows. They spent their lives in prayer, manual labor, and the practice of asceticism.

There were also separate orders of widows whose functions included prayer, the practice of works of charity, and hospitality. In the primitive Church, widowed women could refuse remarriage and become formally invested in a life of celibacy. St. Paul listed the criteria for membership as a minimum age of sixty years and a limit of only one marriage (I Tim. 5:9). He refers to aged women "in holy attire" in his epistle to Titus (Tit. 2:3).

Deaconesses to a certain degree were the female counterparts to deacons—sometimes they were the wives of deacons—consecrated by prayer and a ceremony administered by male clergy. They were required to be "chaste, not slanderers, but sober, [and] faithful in all things" (I Tim 3:11). The First Councils of Nicaea (325) and the Council of Chalcedon (451) established criteria for becoming a deaconess—one requirement was a minimum age of forty. Their consecration prayer contained the following words:

> O eternal God, Father of our Lord Jesus Christ, Creator of man and woman, who didst fill Miriam and Deborah and Hannah and Huldah with the Spirit, and didst not disdain to suffer thine only-begotten Son to be born of a woman; who also in the tabernacle and the temple didst appoint women keepers of thine holy gates: look down now upon this thin handmaid who is designated to the office of deacon, and give her your Holy Spirit. . . .

Deaconesses were installed for the specific purpose of ministering to female catechumens in the Church. They assisted at their baptizing at a time when the process involved full immersion of the near-naked body into water, a rite that would have been awkward for males to administer to females unassisted. Deaconesses were under the jurisdiction of the bishop. The office was abolished by the Synod of Orleans in 533, although deaconesses continued to exist unofficially for several more centuries, particularly in the East.

The Veil

In ancient Rome, a newly married woman donned a veil—either completely red or with a red stripe—to distinguish herself from an unmarried woman. Some pagan cults required men to worship by covering their heads while women did not wear head coverings or shaved their heads entirely. Disheveled hair was another characteristics of cult worship, as evidenced by the followers of Dionysus, and loose, flowing hair was often an integral part of pagan magical formulas. Jewish culture considered loose hair unclean—the mark of the leper or prostitute—and hair was often artfully braided and pinned.[9] Greeks saw the hair as a means of temptation. The Medusa's hair was transformed from beautiful strands to threatening snakes, symbolizing negatively the allure of a woman's tresses. Respectable women in Roman, Jewish, and Greek cultures kept their hair under wraps, removing their sexuality from public display. In some cases, they were veiled even at home, revealing their hair only to their husbands during intimate moments. In Talmudic times, the head covering was so central to married life that for a husband to uncover his wife's head in public was tantamount to an act of divorce.

In many cultures, both the veil and the color of black were believed to repel evil, rendering the wearer invisible to the evil eye. Face and head veiling also had a practical side, protecting the skin and hair from wind and sun, preventing the inhalation of airborne sand particles, and cutting the sun's glare in the eyes. Females have valued smooth, unweathered skin in many eras and have employed veiling to guarantee it.

The veil has appeared in cultures in the majority of ancient and modern civilizations, from China and Korea to Burma and Russia. In the 1960s, when the French tried to force Algerian women to remove their veils, even women who had not worn them previously took them up as a show of nationalism. Similarly, many well-educated modern Iranian women today see the *chador* as a sign of ethnic pride, even though it is not strictly a choice to wear it in most cases. Consumer Studies scholar Susan Michelman noted in a recent article, "There is a current movement in Egypt among lower-middle-class women to re-turn to veiling practices as part of the women's attempt to turn back to a more culturally authentic way of life—a cultural reformation. Westerners quickly perceive this as regression, but they may not have considered more personal issues such as personal identity and social mediation."[10]

In the ancient world, laws frequently compelled married women to wear a veil in public. It is an old practice—records from Assyrian law from 1200 B.C. address the requirement. Slaves and prostitutes, how-ever, were not permitted to wear veils, and a concubine could be veiled only if accompanied by the principal wife. Often veils covered the en-tire face in public. Up to the tenth century, married women wore veils or turbanlike hats in Christian lands. The custom of matrons donning some type of head covering in public lingered many centuries longer, until as late as the nineteenth century in the West.

Some scholars surmise that the motive for St. Paul's biblical in-structions for veiling was a strategic maneuver to ensure that the women of the new Christian Churches were distinguishable from their contemporary pagan counterparts while at the same time remaining within the boundaries of Roman and Jewish custom. Worshipping without a veil or with unbound hair would have been considered taboo by a variety of cultural standards. These historians assert that because St. Paul knew that Christian women would symbolize to the watching world the new religion of Christ, he instituted guidelines regarding their dress, specifically the insistence on the veil during worship, as a purely political move.

In the beginning of his instructive epistles to the Corinthians, where he discussed the rationale behind veiling for women, St. Paul confirmed that he was relaying the commandment of Jesus Christ— that what he advised were not his own ideas. Thus, early Christian women accepted St. Paul's teaching as the directly inspired Word of God and therefore implemented the practice. St. Paul explained that the veil signified the hierarchy that God established in the universe, so when he advised women to cover their heads "because of the angels," he was perhaps referring to the Christian teaching that angels are present at liturgical celebrations.

The biblical passage regarding headship (I Cor. 11:5–16) has been the subject of much discussion in literature, particularly among feminist scholars. Elizabeth Schüssler Fiorenza argues that some aspects of the Bible are to be interpreted within the patriarchal cultural framework of the time in which they were written. Other historians argue that secular veiling was created by men as a means for women's protection against unwanted sexual advances, or even that the Christian veil maintained an earlier Jewish custom of the separation of male and female sites of public worship spaces. There are many other interpretations of the exact meanings of Paul's veiling instructions, but the Church officially required it of women at Mass until the requirement of wearing a head covering in church was dropped in the 1983 Code of Canon Law. However, it remains part of Catholic tradition for many women to continue the practice even today. When Princess Diana, a non-Catholic, visited Pope John Paul II, for example, she chose to wear a traditional black lace mantilla.

St. Ambrose (340–397) referred to the veiling of his sister Marcilla and reasoned that veiled virgins physically decreed their status as Brides of Christ, since all married women wore veils according to ancient tradition. A veil consecration rite was in effect as early as the second century. As a Jewish woman, the Blessed Virgin Mary would have always worn a veil in public, a significant factor in the development of the Christian veil custom. Until recently she was always portrayed veiled in art.

In Greek mythology, Pandora is considered the first bride. The goddess Athena helped her to dress in fine silver clothes, putting on her head a richly embroidered veil, garlands of herbs and flowers, and a golden crown. Brides in secular and religious circles alike have repeated Pandora's preceremony dressing ritual. In fact, the Latin word *nubere* (to marry) also means "to veil oneself."

The veil was the original article of clothing used by Christian consecrated virgins to distinguish themselves from secular society. It signified that, as a Bride of Christ, the wearer was not available for marriage, and was a symbol of her consecration and constancy. Early records exist describing a white veil of probation assigned to novices, a black profession veil, a consecrated veil given specifically to virgins at the age of twenty-five, a veil presented to deaconesses at age forty, a veil taken specifically by widows, and a veil of penitence. Many of these veils later became obsolete.

The first Christian virgins either took the veil themselves or received it in a ritual from their parents. They wore it continually, not reserving it just for worship. Widows who consecrated themselves to chastity also took the veil. After a short time, the solemn consecration of virgins, called the *velatio,* was performed only by bishops and priests, and they alone bestowed the veil to virgins and widows. In the *Roman Pontifical,* the rite for the consecration of virgins closely parallels the ceremony of priestly ordination. Here the gift of the veil is accompanied by these words: "Receive the sacred veil, that thou mayst be known to have despised the world, and to be truly humble, and with all thy heart subject to Christ as His Bride; and may He defend thee from all evil, and bring thee to life eternal."

The veil, then, has always been considered as the most significant piece of the habit. Of all the blessed garments, the original veil given at profession was so tenderly regarded that it was often preserved for the nun's burial. Medieval illustrations portray English abbess Lucy of Hedingham carried to heaven by an angel, naked of earthly clothing except for her black veil. Although by no means the only sign of consecration, it has held a special place and power among the components of the habit. Tradition holds that Christ's friend Veronica wiped His brow with her veil on the Via Dolorosa (route upon which Christ carried the cross), whereby it became imprinted with an image of His face. When sparks from a burning outbuilding threatened the convent of Nivelles, the spirit of its foundress Gertrude was observed on the roof, shielding it with her veil.[11] Today many sisters who wear secular clothing still continue to wear the religious veil.

The male monastic counterpart to the veil is the cowl, possibly originating in the East as a representation of the innocence and simplicity of a child's hood. In the ninth century, one of the Councils of Aachen described a veiling period for men that lasted three days, originating as a sign of admission into community. Later this three-day period took on symbolic meaning, representing the three days Christ descended to hell during His Passion.

Monks also received the distinct haircut called the tonsure. This practice is thought to have originated from the custom of cutting the hair of slaves. Typically it involved a shaven skull except for a fringe of hair around the perimeter of the hairline. It became symbolic of Christ's crown of thorns, and variations of the design signified membership of particular orders. Similarly, the early nuns of Egypt and Syria cut off their hair, a gesture of destroying earthly vanity not commonly practiced in the West until centuries later. It was not mentioned in regulations until the thirteenth century.

Hair, considered by Christians as the glory of a woman's head, was offered as a sacrifice to God, symbolizing a pledge of chastity. It is a ceremony reminiscent of early Greek pagans, who cut off their hair as a sacrificial act. Later, short hair became a matter of convenience more than anything, although many orders continue to employ a symbolic cutting of a lock of hair at the profession ceremony. The Poor Clare Colentines still follow their old custom of shearing their hair completely at profession, placing the shorn hair in a basket with a crucifix, which is left in the chapel the entire day of the vestition.

Church Fathers

By A.D. 100, when there were an estimated twenty thousand Christians, Church customs and manners began to become formally unified.[12] Church Father Tertullian (140–230) gave a comprehensive overview of rules for female attire in many of his writings, detailing the clothing, hair, and makeup customs of his time and what should be employed or avoided. Tertullian would not endear himself to many women today. In blaming Eve, and subsequently all of the female sex, for the fall of the human race from the Grace of God, Tertullian's theories of dress reflected his underlying hypothesis that due to the enormity of Eve's mistake, all women should shun decorative dress and don penitential garb.

Of the veil, he advised, "Arabia's heathen females will be your judges, who cover not only the head but the face also, so entirely that they are content with only one eye free, to enjoy rather half the light than to prostitute the entire face." He urged virgins to veil themselves because they are "the devil's gateway," expressing a concept that has carried through even today—that women act as temptresses through their choice of dress, rendering men helpless and unaccountable for predatory or even violent actions.

Tertullian expounded in great detail on the frivolity of gold, silver, and jewels: "Even though we call this thing a pearl, it certainly must be seen to be nothing else but a hard and round lump inside a shellfish." He also frowned on the use of imported goods: "the only thing that gives glamour to all these articles is that they are rare and that they have been imported from a foreign country." He was a strong proponent of naturally colored fibers: "We cannot suppose that God was unable to produce sheep with purple or sky-blue fleeces . . . hence, they must be understood to be from the Devil, who is the corrupter of nature," and stressed simplicity and dignity in dress.

Tertullian emphasized the importance of external modesty from internal motives and reasoned that Christian women should try to distinguish both their appearance and their morality from those of pagans. He defined Christian modesty as "hating to be the object of desire of another." Tertullian argued that if a woman preferred to be free from lust herself, why would she wish to present a stumbling block to others through her appearance? He quoted Christ's words "thou shalt love they neighbor as thyself" as the most important reason for dressing modestly and found no good reason for a woman to enhance her physical beauty before or after marriage, suggesting that a husband should love his wife for her character alone. He counseled women to strive for a "natural and demure neatness" instead. Here many women would agree.

On makeup, he opined, "surely those women sin against God who anoint their faces with creams, stain their cheeks with rouge, or lengthen their eyebrows with antimony. Obviously, they are not satisfied with the creative skill of God . . . in their own person." On hair, he stated, "I see some women dye their hair blonde by using saffron. They are even ashamed of their country, sorry that they were not born in Germany or Gaul!" He advised, "as a matter of fact, the strength of these bleaches really does harm to the hair . . . just as the warmth of the sun, while desirable for giving life and dryness to the hair, if overdone is hurtful." Of covering gray hair, he noted, "the harder we work to conceal our age the more we reveal it," and he described the "crime against simplicity" of curls, braids, elaborate chignons, wigs, and hairpieces. He summarized his opinions by reminding women that they would not be able to take their headgear and makeup to heaven, so "why not let God see you today as He will on your day of judgement?" Men were not excluded from his tirades on appearance. In the same essay, he expressed his disturbance over males with fancifully shaven beards or inappropriate hair lengths and berated those who exfoliated their skin with pumice grit or who gazed anxiously in the mirror at the first sign of gray hair.

On clothing, Tertullian cautioned women against "a lot of frilly and foolish pomp and luxury." He argued that "people only wear fancy dress in public ... to be seen." He recommended that clothing should be appropriate for the occasion, and one's tasks should reflect one's holiness. Thus, Christians had no need of fine clothes for visiting the sick or attending Mass or any other activity worthy of Christian behavior. He suggested wearing clothes that gave evidence to the Faith, such as the veil, alluding to the laws that forbade prostitutes to wear veils due to their impure status. His final word on the apparel of women recommended, "so great and abundant [should be] your modesty that it may flow from the mind to the garb."

Another important patristic document regarding female Christian dress was St. Cyprian of Carthage's (200–258) "On the Dress of Virgins." Like Tertullian, he stressed modesty in dress and adornment. Cyprian considered that "no one on seeing a virgin should be in any doubt as to whether she is one." He further argued that a woman's physical strength or the "tortures she might endure for Christ" were far superior to her appearance. He also addressed wealthy women specifically, advising them to use their riches for God rather than their own decoration. He referred to the Great Whore of the Apocalypse, described by St. John as "that woman ... arrayed in a purple and scarlet mantle." Cyprian advised virgins against wearing jewelry and to be recognized by "the conspicuous plainness of [their] attire." He suggested that virgins avoid wedding banquets and public bathhouses, where "nakedness destroys one's modesty," and reminded them of the benefits of virginity—that they would not have the pains of childbirth or a husband to rule over them, comparing their virginal lives to those of "the angels of God."

Clement of Alexandria (d. 215) attributed the desire to own more clothes than necessary to a specific weakness in women. Clement also referred to the diaphanous materials of the dresses of prostitutes and advised women against wearing such clothing that excited lust by revealing the female figure.[13] He reasoned that men and women should not regard each other as sex objects and should choose dress befitting of brothers and sisters in Christ. It is important to note that while many of the Church Fathers often are labeled as misogynistic in their formal writings about women, their attitudes toward women as seen in letters to mothers, sisters, and friends is quite often respectful and warm. Perhaps what may seem obsessive or puritanical to modern sensibilities may have been entirely appropriate for the times.

Penance

The austere and penitential nature of the habit was of a deliberate theological design. St. Luke recorded Christ's words: "Except you do penance, you shall all likewise perish." Penance may be described as the hatred of sin as an offense against God and a firm purpose of amendment and satisfaction. One object of monastic life, then, was to make reparations for personal sins as well as for the sins of all humankind. Many believed that the Second Coming of Christ was at hand and withdrew entirely from the world to prepare for it. By finding ways to participate in Christ's Passion, believers thought they would better ensure their place in His Heavenly kingdom, thus explaining their willingness to embrace suffering.

Hebrew rites of penance and mourning began with the rending of garments, symbolic of returning to primitive nakedness. The penitent clothed himself in sackcloth, a fabric typically used to cover a corpse. He lay on the ground and sprinkled his body with dust and ashes to reinforce this symbolism. Christians also used clothes as a means of self-mortification and penitential exercises. Some early ascetics of the desert chose to wear inadequate clothing as an act of penance. Others denied themselves comfort by donning only garb made of coarse, chafing materials such as a hairshirt. This was a garment made of rough cloth derived from bristly goat's hair and worn in the form of a chemise over the torso or as a girdle around the loins, for the specific purpose of causing pain or irritation. In Latin it was called a *cilicium*, named from the city of Cilicia, where it was believed to have originated.

St. John the Baptist wore a garment of camel's hair and a leather belt, a combination that became his trademark and was reminiscent of the garb of the Old Testament prophets Elijah and Elisha. This apparel evolved into an early form of monastic dress made of skins secured with a leather belt called the *melota*. The belt symbolically divides the body into an upper, spiritual section and a lower, sexual one.

Penitential clothing served to aid in resisting the temptations of the flesh—the discomfort constantly reminded the wearer of his or her need to overcome earthly desires for Christ's sake. It also allowed the user to directly experience the sufferings of the Lord, in imitation of Him. Laypersons, particularly those who lived in luxury, used the hairshirt as extensively as religious brothers and sisters to combat their otherwise comfortable lifestyles. Domnina (d. 460) was an ascetic in Syria. Theodoret of Cyrrus (393–466) tells us that she set up a small hut in her parents' garden to maintain solitude but remained supported by her parents. She wore uncomfortable clothing made from hair and a hood that covered her face.[14]

In the canonization process of St. Margaret of Hungary (1242–1271), St. Mary of the Isle reported:

> St. Margaret used to wear clothes in which there were a lot of lice, and when she took these clothes off, she did not want the lice to be removed. For a time she wore on her back a fur with more lice in it than you could possibly tell, and she did not want the lice removed from it. Asked how she knew this, she replied, "Because I saw it, and I often ran away from her [St. Margaret] because of the lice." Asked why she wore clothes with so many lice in it and did not want them removed, she replied, "So that it would be a greater penance."[15]

Charlemagne (742–814) was buried in the hairshirt he wore during his lifetime, and for many centuries all penitents wore haircloth on Ash Wednesday. In the Sarum Rite, used in pre-Reformation England,

Scotland, and Ireland, a haircloth banner was carried in procession on Maundy Thursday, and the altar was sometimes covered with haircloth during the penitential season of Lent. In the Middle Ages, penitential garments were sometimes made of wire. The belt or cincture was also used as an instrument of penance, with its wearer tightening it to the point of discomfort. Some penitents even wore pointed hoods completely covering the face except for an opening for the eyes. This practice continued until at least the Middle Ages, as illustrated by an eighteenth-century drawing showing a medieval nun from the Third Order of Saint Francis wearing such a device.

Holy Individuals

Jesus said if one wished to attain eternal life, it was better to renounce one's possessions than to keep them. St. Matthew recorded, "If thou wilt be perfect, go sell what thou hast, and give to the poor," and St. Paul quoted in his first letter to the Corinthians, "you are not your own." Christ taught that man cannot satisfy his nature with temporal goods and at the same time retain an appetite for the eternal. He was the ultimate example of perfect self-denial, offering this path to holiness: "If any man will come after me, let him deny himself."

In Egypt, the first monks believed that renunciation of earthly goods should be made as absolute as possible. "Adamites" threw off their clothes entirely. The rule of those who did wear clothing was that it had to be so poor and wretched that no one would steal it if it was left lying around. Others lived on extremely small amounts of food and water and experimented with various forms of seemingly eccentric forms of hermit life, residing in trees or atop pillars.

The solitary life attracted many Christians, particularly in times of persecution. Typically, a person would seek out an elder and ask to be instructed in his or her holy ways. The religious person's possessions typically consisted only of a coarse mat, a sheepskin, a lamp, and containers for water and oil. Some desert holy women may not have worn veils, but they hid themselves away from others and maintained rigorous privacy. Alexandra of Egypt is noted to have shut herself away in a mausoleum in the fourth century, putting up a curtain in the tiny window to avoid anyone seeing her face.[16]

By the third century, male and female Christian ascetics were living in Egypt, Syria, Palestine, Caesarea, Spain, Mesopotamia, and Persia. Some groups resided in the desert, while others were located in cities. A fifth-century bishop of Palladus spent years in the Egyptian desert and recorded seeing as many as twenty thousand female ascetics there, outnumbering men by a ratio of two to one.[17] Early female ascetics spent their days in prayer, penitential exercises, and manual labor. They bathed infrequently, wore poor clothing, and some shunned shoes. For those from wealthy backgrounds and even royal heritage, these were marked departures from societal norms.

By the end of the third century, celibate women grouped together to form the beginnings of the great medieval monasteries and religious orders of the Middle Ages. By the fourth century, there are references to ascetics, virgins, widows, deaconesses, ammas (desert mothers), nuns, and canonesses.[18] Because Christianity was not the official religion of the Roman Empire until late in the fourth century, it is unlikely that the nun's habit originated in its earliest years as an imposition by the Church, as one might assume. Instead, various women demonstrated strong attachment to their religious garb. Over time, these garments became emblems of community as the cenobitic or communal life superseded the eremitic one. Initially, however, the nun's habit was simply a voluntary action of individual holiness, a choice by its wearer outwardly to mark her path to saintliness. The courageous sisters of the early Church made their own decisions regarding appearance, and the heroism of these first virgins and martyrs has been celebrated in the liturgy, statuary, and stained glass of Catholicism for centuries. They pioneered new standards for their gender within a religion that would overtake all others by the end of the next era.

CHAPTER FOUR

Conformity

The first monks and nuns were more concerned with individual ascetic perfection than with solemnizing their way of life through formal
ceremony and community consensus. Early Christianity was a time of
experimentation, and the characteristics of religious life varied widely.
Still, it was a Church filled with rituals and sacramental objects. The
ceremonial changing of clothing continued to serve as a primary means
in which religious declared their calling, whereby the inner person was
transformed with outer signs. Taking on special apparel was viewed as
a second baptism, cleansing and transforming the inner and outer person. One desert father wrote, "I have seen the power which I have seen
standing over baptism also over the vestment of a monk when he received the spiritual habit."[1]

The phrase "taking the habit" was from earliest times synonymous
with becoming a religious person. The new clothing permanently re-
oriented life and marked the wearer. By the sixth century, religious men
and women were visibly identifiable by their garb, whether living in
community or alone as hermits. In the eleventh century, St. Anselm
(d. 1109), the Archbishop of Canterbury, wrote to King Harold's
daughter, Gunnilda:

> For although you were not consecrated by a bishop and did
> not read a profession in his presence, the fact that you publicly

and privately wore the habit of the holy way of life, by which you proclaimed to all who saw you that you were dedicated to God no less than by reading a profession, is in itself a manifest and undeniable profession. . . .[2]

For many monks and nuns of the Middle Ages, the holy habit was their only assertion of religious life; many never took formal vows. This tacit profession is one that would linger on in some cases until the nineteenth century.

The communal way of life added a new dimension to the habit, however. From the beginning, the Catholic Church has been a hierarchical organization. It taught that Christ conferred on its leadership the right to legislate when He bestowed the keys of the Kingdom of Heaven to his apostle Peter, the first pope. This is the Church's claim of authority and why its monarchical and patriarchal system has remained unchanged to this day. Christ stated: "And if he will not hear the church, let him be to thee as the heathen and the publican" (Matt. 18:17). Thus, Catholics pledge allegiance to the authority of the Church when they become formal members.

St. Matthew recorded Jesus Christ's words: "If any man will come after me, let him deny himself and take up his cross and follow me." Beginning with early monastic groups, religious persons pledged obedience not only to the will of God but to their superior and the community. Although some orders incorporated a general chapter system, where issues were discussed and decided on—or an even more democratic form of self-governance—the individual relinquished his or her personal desires for those of the community. If an order developed a special dress code or habit, the monks and nuns were strictly bound to wear it or be excommunicated from the community. Even after becoming pope, Benedict XII (d. 1342) continued to wear his monk's cowl as often as his papal duties would permit. From the very moment postulants sought admittance into a community, they subsumed their individuality in that of the group. Some orders did not permit a monastic to own his or her clothes—the garments were common property, permanently on loan. This compliance fostered unity and harmony and had an important spiritual dimension as well, expanding the habit beyond an exterior gauge of personal commitment into one of group conformity.

Earliest Monastic Habits

Pachomius (ca. 292–356) is recognized as the founder of the first monastery. His sister, Mary, directed a house of over four hundred women who followed a rule for living designed by Pachomius. He called it the *Rule of the Angel*, because he asserted that an angel had dictated it to him. Paula (347–404), another of the early great abbesses, and her daughter, Eustochium (368–420), founded convents near Bethlehem following the same rule. Paula was the great friend and intellectual companion of the Church Father St. Jerome (340–420). Segregated into three separate classifications, the nuns at Paula's convent at Bethlehem dressed identically. Their clothing was generally made from wool, an ideal fabric for austere monasteries that were cold in winter and damp in summer, with linen being used only for drying hands. Paula taught her sisters that "a clean body and a clean dress mean an unclean soul" and prohibited the type of bathing and narcissistic care for the body that prevailed in pagan culture. She instituted a rigorous communal schedule for labor, fasting, and prayer.[3]

In Pachomian monasteries, males replaced the *melota* of the desert with the Roman tunic and *pallium*, and wore an apronlike scapular to protect the tunic while performing manual labor. The earliest tunics from the ancient world featured a side opening that required a belt for closure. They were made from linen or wool, according to climate. Both Roman and Jewish worship ceremonies required participants to be clad in scrupulously clean clothes, so white linen became widely used in sacred places because it is a material that becomes whiter with continued washing and wear. Originally only women wore the floor-length version of the tunic, while men wore a shorter style. But the long tunic evolved into an acceptable male garment, worn by pagan gods and heroes.[4] Later both the men and women of Christianity would adopt it. Eventually the tunic fell out of fashion in pagan culture and was worn only by servants. Yet Christians, the "Servants of God," would continue to wear it for generations to come.

For Christians, the tunic's T shape was reminiscent of the Cross of Calvary. Making the sign of the cross has always been one of the most powerful rituals in Catholicism, representing both the life and death of Christ. For monastics, donning the tunic was to clothe oneself in the mystery of the Passion. Paul the Hermit, a legendary contemporary of St. Anthony and considered the first Christian desert eremite, was said to have woven a tunic for himself in the desert from palm leaves. A tenth-century writer compared the tunic's width to the love of behaving well, its length to the perseverance of adhering firmly, and its height to the contemplation of celestial life. It was often referred to as the uniform of the "Soldier of Christ"—referring back to St. Paul's metaphor (II Tim. 2:3).[5]

Over the tunic, some monks adopted the Roman *pallium*, known as the garment of philosophers. But the scapular, a word derived from the Latin *scapula*, for shoulder, would become one of the most essential elements of both the nun's and monk's habit for years to come. It was originally T-shaped with cross-bands underneath the arms and was often called simply a "cross." It was made from a piece of cloth the width of the breast from shoulder to shoulder, not quite reaching to the ground in front or behind. Expressly spoken of in the Rule of St. Benedict, sometimes the scapular featured a hood fastened at the back. It is the most external item of the habit, which is why it evolved into an important community identifier. Its color could denote a nun's or a monk's community or the wearer's status within the community. The Benedictine scapular was black. Later Cistercians and Dominicans adopted white to symbolize purity and innocence, while Franciscans and Carmelites wore brown to symbolize poverty and lowliness.[6] Today a layperson may wear, under the clothing, a small version of various scapulars that are associated with specific confraternities or privileges. The Green Scapular carries with it the Virgin Mary's intercession in effecting conversions or cures. Monks also wore the *cuculla* (hooded cape), onto which Pachomius requested they sew a purple fabric cross. This cape became such a distinctive mark of the religious man that in the Middle Ages monks were often referred to as the *gens cuculatta* (people of the cape).

Basil of Caesarea (329–379), considered the patriarch of monks in the East, required his brothers to wear a belt, citing as example Christ's girding himself before he washed his disciples' feet. The only requirement for receiving the habit in Eastern communities was a brief period of examination. For four or five days, a monk would be assigned unpleasant household tasks in order to test his humility and patience. If he passed, he was instructed briefly in the religious life and then vested in the community garb. The new monk's secular clothes were kept in case he later decided to leave or if he was expelled.

St. Basil proposed that women had the same potential for ascetic perfection as males. He probably influenced his sister, the great abbess Macrina the Younger (330–379), who established a female monastery in northeast Asia Minor, to choose a distinctive dress "of sombre color." When Macrina died, her female associates searched her things to find something to adorn her body for burial, but all they could find was a tunic, veil, and shabby sandals. Preparing her body, they found around her neck an iron cross and ring, fastened with a cord, which they removed for future generations to cherish.[7]

Back in the West, Marcella (325–410) was a wealthy Roman patrician woman who caused quite a stir when she donned religious garb. She was another of Jerome's friends, and because of her status as a powerful ruling matron from an illustrious marriage, her peers initially scorned her austere new clothing. Jerome wrote that her action was considered "strange and . . . ignominious and degrading." But attitudes soon changed, and her decision influenced others of her rank to join her in adopting similar clothing, including Marcellina, the sister of St. Ambrose, who received her veil directly from Pope Liberius in 353.

Jerome wrote extensively about clothing to his female friends—his best-known letters on the lifestyle of the virgin were written to Eustochium. These letters condemned all but chaste and ascetic lives, employing discussion about clothing to convey literal and metaphorical lessons on female virtue. Jerome spoke of women who "donned dark dress" and exchanged their finery for plainer attire. In one letter, he detailed the decision of a young woman to enter religious life in spite of opposition from her family:

> . . . she cast from her the ornaments of her person and her secular dress, as if they were encumbrances to her resolve. Costly necklaces, precious pearls, brilliant jewels, she replaces in their cabinet; she puts on a common tunic, and over it a more common cloak; and without giving any notice, suddenly throws herself at her grandmother's knees, showing who she was only by weeping and lamentation. Aghast was that holy and venerable lady, seeing the altered dress of her grandchild; while her mother stood astounded. . . .

Jerome wrote of another friend, Asella, who decided to dress in dark clothes and sold a valuable golden necklace and gave the money to the poor. To his friend Furia he wrote:

> Would that men would imitate the laudable examples of women, and that wrinkled old age would pay at last what youth gladly offers first! . . . If we are widows, we must either speak as we are dressed, or else dress as we speak. . . . The tongue talks of chastity, but the body reveals incontinence. . . .

Exchange your love of necklaces and of gems and of silk dresses for earnestness in studying the scriptures.

He advised his friend Demetrias to "shun the frivolity of girls who wear hair ornaments, let their hair fall in a fringe over their forehead, who use face-cream and cosmetics to improve their skins, and who go in for tight sleeves, dresses without a crease, and slippers with curled up toes." In other letters, he warned against putting on pious dress as a sign of modesty when true virtue was absent.

Another of the fourth-century fathers, St. John Chrysostom (344–407), spoke and wrote specifically about women's clothing. He observed that the nuns of his time wore a black tunic bound together by a girdle, a white veil on their forehead, and a black mantle, which covered the head and the entire body. If worn, shoes were pointed and white. He praised teenage girls who for the sake of Christianity "laid aside their soft clothing" and went shoeless, but chastised those who did not adopt simple and modest dress:

> That is why Elijah, that is why John had simple clothes; they threw tunics of skins and a haircloth cloak around themselves, since they longed for, they desired to receive the garment of immortality. But you even exceed those women on the stage in attentiveness to your couture, through which you display devices wildly to excite young men. Not thus does the Bridegroom wish you to be adorned and beautiful; instead he has commanded that all your glory be deposited in your soul. But you neglect the soul and ornament the mud and ashes in diverse ways; you drag along with you dissolute lovers, making adulterers, as they say, of all who see you. That you kindle a great fire, I do not think you will deny.[8]

The Holy Rule

The first monastic rules were generally suitable for both women and men. The Holy Rule was a formal plan for day-to-day living, often written or dictated by an esteemed Church leader, and followed implicitly by a community. The Rule of St. Augustine was first written by Augustine (354–430) for his small band of monks in Hippo, North Africa. Later he adapted it for nuns with almost no changes beyond the substitution of feminine for masculine pronouns.

After Augustine's death, various communities of nuns in southern Europe adopted his rule, adding their own clarifications to the original, such as the recommendation to avoid "such delicate headcoverings that your hairnets show through."[9] The rule alluded to there being a specific nun in charge of wardrobe, suggesting that she choose attire that was unassuming and neither expensive nor immodest. Augustine's rule also offered detailed advice regarding maintenance:

> Have your clothing under the care of one or two women, or however many as may be needed for shaking them so that the moths do not damage them. Just as you are fed from one store-room, so you should be clothed from one closet. And if it is possible, do not be concerned what clothing appropriate to the season is supplied you, whether each individual received the garment that she has turned in or another garment that someone else has worn, as long as each woman is not denied what she needs....[10]

As a contemporary of Augustine, St. Patrick (387–493) brought Christianity northward to Ireland, where it flourished. A metaphorical early Irish monastic motto was "Be always naked in imitation of Christ and the Evangelists." Born in 543, the Irish saint Columbanus wrote a monastic rule that emphasized obedience, silence, abstinence from food, poverty, humility, and chastity. It included prescriptions for rigorous fasting, various types of manual labor, and an undyed woolen habit and cowl. Columbanus was particularly focused on the spiritual equality of women, and females participated to a great extent in early Irish monasticism. St. Brigid (451–525), who once sang and played the harp for kings in Ireland, founded the first female Christian monastery in 480. She defied her parents to aid the mission of St. Patrick, taking the veil at a very early age and building a hermit's cell in an oak tree. Her monastery at Kildare gave the town its name, which in the Irish language is known as Cill Dara, or "the church of the oak."

Irish nuns provided shelter for traveling monks; manufactured vestments, altar cloths, and books; and taught religion to children. In Ireland, women who wished to live as consecrated virgins found great opposition from their families and communities. As it was difficult for them to live an ascetic lifestyle individually at home, they chose to band together in monastic groups early on. Brigid was responsible for this rapid spread of female monasticism in her day, and she organized monasteries with a distinct tradition that would last for many centuries. Although it is not known for certain, it is believed that her nuns wore a white tunic and black mantle.

In Gaul, St. Caesarius (470–543), the Bishop of Arles, wrote a rule exclusively directed to women for his sister Caesaria, who was leader at the monastery of St. John. He presented it at the group's foundation, specifying that the women should experiment to find which parts were "in harmony with reason and possible with sanctity." It was therefore a collaborative effort.

Clothing historian Desiree Koslin notes that because cloth dyeing involved relying on outside professional help, it was not befitting for the humble status of the monastic and was prohibited at the monastery. Chapters 44 and 45 of Caesarius's rule stated: "Let them have all their clothing only in simple and respectable color, never black, never bright white, but only natural or milky white . . . and let nothing be added to these other than crosses, either black or white, and only of plain work from scraps of cloths or linens." At this time, cloth spun from the wool of all-white flocks was rare and expensive. In the same manner, pure black materials would have been reserved for wealthy consumers because of its required flock selectivity and dyeing procedures. Monastic garb from undyed fabric could have reflected a variety of hues from light pink to rich reddish brown, depending on the natural fleece from which the fabric was made.[11] Nuns were obliged to make their clothing completely by their own hands, and it could be neither quilted nor embroidered. They cared for each other's clothes and polished each other's shoes.

In addition to textile work, Caesarius advised nuns to take up book production as a means of earning money. The original rule later evolved into another version, called the *Rule for Nuns.* These regulations required literacy and for religious women to spend two hours a day on intellectual pursuits. Fasting and recitation of the Divine Office were other stipulations.[12] The rule even addressed the manner in which nuns tied up their hair. Early abbesses also stressed the importance of physical enclosure to focus their nuns' attention inward and to eliminate distractions from the world.

St. Benedict's famous rule was written sometime around 530. Benedict of Nursia (ca. 480–ca. 550) was noted for not demanding anything of others that he had not experienced himself as a monk, and his regulations discouraged private asceticism and encouraged community life. The Rule of St. Benedict served to Westernize and modify many Eastern ascetic traditions, and it is widely followed even today. St. Benedict addressed all areas of life—silence, prayer, discipline, food, travel, and hospitality, with a special emphasis on labor and obedience. He prohibited private ownership except by express permission from the abbot, and although written for men, the rule would be adopted by women as well. Chapter 55 related specifically to the clothing of monks:

> Suitable clothing shall be given to all monks, dependent on the climate. In cold regions more will be required than in warm. All this will be decided by the abbot. However, in temperate

regions, we believe that each monk will make do with a cowl and tunic—heavy for winter, light (or worn) for summer. He should also have a shift for labor and shoes for the feet.

Monks shall not complain of the color or texture of their clothing. It shall be whatever is available in the surrounding countrysides or whatever is cheapest.

The abbot shall see to fit so that the clothes are not too short but properly sized to the wearer. When new clothes are handed out, the monks shall turn in their old ones. These will be stored in the wardrobe for the poor. Each monk needs only two each of tunics and cowls, so he will be prepared for night wear and washing. Anything else is superfluous and should be banished. Shoes and other garments will also be returned when replaced. Those who must travel will be given leggings. Afterwards these are to be washed and returned. On these trips they should have better quality cowls and tunics than usual; these are to be returned after use.

Bedding shall consist of a mattress, coverlet, blanket and pillow. The abbot will make frequent inspections of the bedding to prevent hoarding. Any infractions are subject to the severest discipline and, so that this vice of private ownership may be cut away at the roots, the abbot is to furnish all necessities: cowl, tunic, shoes, stockings, belt, knife, pen, needle, towel and writing tablet. With these, any excuse for need will be vanquished.

The abbot must always remember, "And distribution was made to every one, according as he had need" (Acts 4:35). He should take into account the frailties of those in need and not the hostility of the envious. In everything he should think of the retribution of God.

The most important aspect of Benedictine clothing was that it was chosen by another—the abbott or abbess—and was not the property of the monk. Given that the Benedictine rule gave directions for distributing worn-out clothing to the poor, it could not have differed so much from that worn by secular society.[13] However, Benedict would have considered it essential that the entire monastic ensemble appear distinctive—accomplished through the use of extremely coarse and low-grade material at a time when differences in quality of fabric were of great significance in society. Benedict also insisted on monks wearing finer clothing for traveling so that they would not appear conspicuously poor as an attempt to gain sympathy or alms. Regarding shoes, Benedict's mentioned *"pedules et caligas,"* which could have meant stockings, socks, or light indoor footwear and sandals. The abbot and pope St. Gregory the Great (ca. 540–604) wrote of nailed boots worn for work at this time.[14] New shoes typically were distributed at the feast of Michaelmas (celebrated September 29).

Early Benedictines commonly wore undyed clothing. Although Benedict's rule did not specify anything about color, Benedictines later became known as "black monks" or "black nuns" when they adopted dyed black clothing, perhaps to symbolize the color of separateness, mourning, and penance—symbolism that was not always recognized as such in the Middle Ages. At times, black was actually considered a color of fashion in secular society. Benedictine tunics were long and flowing, resembling those worn by the Roman upper levels of society except for their fabric, which was of a far cheaper quality. Monks wore a scapular for work and a wide-sleeved *cucullus* for more formal occasions, such as chanting in choir. They slept fully clothed when they shared common rooms, although after individual cells or cubicles were introduced, monks might have chosen to wear less clothing at night.[15] Benedict's sister Scholastica, considered the first Benedictine nun, specified plain attire for her nuns as a sign of poverty and of the way of life they had chosen.

Abbesses

The male-oriented structure of the Church did not preclude females from exercising leadership, and many early monastic communities were ruled over by an abbess, an office defined as the female superior of a community of twelve or more. The title "abbess" was originally of Benedictine origin. Many prominent Christian women served as abbesses and came from wealthy and noble families. Pachomius and Benedict insisted on separation for men and women in monastic communities, yet common houses marked by male and female wings, called double monasteries, also existed. Some abbesses supervised double houses that contained thousands of monks and nuns. This arrangement was prohibited in 787 at the Second Council of Niacea, although it continued to exist among the hospital orders as late as the twelfth century.

Those whom the abbess supervised elected her for a life term. She exercised supreme domestic authority over her monastery and all of its dependents, and she received a solemn benediction at her investiture. Unlike an abbot, her male counterpart, she had no spiritual dominion. However, she could hear a nonsacramental confession and administer punishments, appoint her own administrators, approve confessors for the laity, and confer the veil on virgins.

The office of abbess was the highest leadership position a woman could hold in society. These religious "monarchs" were addressed as "Sovereign" and "Majesty" and enjoyed great power. In England, kings looked to both abbesses and abbots for assistance in the defense of the country. During the reign of Henry I (1068–1135), the Abbess of Shrewsbury organized seven knights to serve her king. At gatherings of Parliament, abbesses participated alongside abbots and bishops, sometimes adding their signatures to charters and documents formulated at these assemblies. They were present at all important national and religious celebrations and moved in all of the same social and political circles as the highest-ranking officials in the land.

Like bishops and abbots, abbesses wore the mitre and the ring of office and carried the staff, sometimes called the crozier. At the installation of the Abbess of St. Cecilia's in Cologne, each member of the clergy under her jurisdiction paid her public homage, prostrating himself before her and kissing her hand.[16] This gesture was a common practice that became modified over the years, lasting well into the eighteenth century. It was abolished entirely in 1750, when the office of abbess lost most of its other privileges.

Bishops, nobles, kings, and queens founded many of the early monasteries. Families of government and Church authorities were often related to the directors of the great abbeys, and their wealth flowed between them. Often secular female nobles and royals had their portraits painted with habited nuns of the congregations they chose to patronize; sometimes they were even portrayed wearing the habits themselves. Families and patrons believed they could exert their influence in the administrative practices of the abbeys.

Medieval Nuns

Bishop Leander of Seville (ca. 540–ca. 600) composed a rule for his abbess sister Florentina advising the following:

> Do not wear stunning clothes, anything having a pleat, for the eye is curious before and behind, and do not wear dresses that billow. Be careful of clothes carefully and diligently patterned and bought at a very high price, for that is the care of the flesh, that is the eager desire of the eyes ... use garments that cover the body, that conceal the maidenly decorum ... that keep out the rigors of cold; not those that produce the incentive and capacity for lust.[17]

Leander's comments alluded to the secular styles of the day. Beginning in the fifth century, lay clothing started to evolve toward covering the body more fully and became more elaborately decorative, often employing the colors and designs of the East. Women wore long tunics topped with short-sleeved robes along with bands of fabric draped over their shoulders. Clothing was often embroidered, and the affluent encrusted their cloth with jewels. Local wools and linens gave way to silks and cottons from China and Egypt. Wealthy society used fabrics often richly patterned with decorative scenes, and the color purple continued to be reserved for the rich or for royalty.

During the Merovingian era in France (481–752), typical aristocratic females wore a silk tunic decorated with bands of embroidery, a scarf draped around the shoulders, a wide belt, and long, loose hair under a white waist-length veil. A sixth-century Merovingian queen was found in an excavated tomb dress wearing a linen shift, a knee-length undertunic of violet silk, jeweled belt, long outer tunic of dark red silk slit open in the front and closed with jeweled pins, gartered linen stockings, and thin leather slippers. The Frankish queen Radegund (ca. 518), however, sought instruction from local hermits in the ways of religious life—one holy woman sent her a hairshirt to wear secretly under her royal robes.[18] If Radegund's attendants praised a new veil as particularly beautiful, she would immediately remove it from her head and send it off to be used as a cloth on the holy altar. Radegund so wished to live as a nun, she later abandoned her husband, the king, to found the convent of the Holy Cross at Poitiers.

Radegund's successor at the abbey did not seem to follow her ascetic footsteps. Two nuns organized a rebellion against the new abbess because she had made a silk dress for her niece from the altar cloth. They also charged the abbess with keeping company with a man in the abbey whom she had disguised in women's clothes.[19]

Similar abuses were observed in other convents. Aldheml, in his work *De Virginitate*, written in the late seventh or early eighth century, reprimanded nuns at Barking in southern England for wearing red-and-blue tunics, sleeves with purple silk stripes, and either garments or shoes (the translation is unclear) that were encircled in red fur. He also mentioned with disapproval that the nuns crimped their hair with a curling iron and used their dark gray veils to hide white and colored veils underneath, the latter hanging down to their ankles.

In the eighth century, secular Christian women continued to wear head coverings, although they began to vary from the standard, simple veil. Sometimes they donned a close-fitting cap that allowed the hair to show in the front. Wealthier women wore hats with padded or rolled edges, usually covered by a cloak hood or veil. The fragments of veils that exist from this period indicate that they were made of fine linen wool, almost gauzy in thickness. Veils were pinned to caps or fastened with fillets or ribbons. Wealthy Christian ladies also wore elaborate jeweled necklaces, often fashioned from gold, amethysts, and garnets in the shape of a cross. The typical shoe was either ankle high, fastened with laces, or a low slipper. They continued wearing an undertunic and overtunic combination, although these began to be modified, with round neck openings and wide, decorated sleeves. It was common to wear personal items suspended from a braided tie-style belt, including small metal containers of relics, combs, keys, and sewing items. Clearly, some religious women continued to follow secular fashions, as a Church council decreed in 787: "Time shall be devoted more to reading books and chanting psalms than to weaving and decorating clothes with various colors in unprofitable richness."

By the ninth century, those women who could be considered religious fell into a variety of categories: consecrated virgins, nuns bound by public religious profession, deaconesses, wives of men from religious orders, and widows. Sometimes young children were pledged to religious service by their parents. These young girls, called oblates, were often bound to religious life without any participation in the decision. In committing these children to God, the parents believed they would share in the sanctity of their children's lives. Some followed the custom of offering the tenth child to religious service, a sort of human tithe.

However, their taking the veil and making simple vows was considered different from pledging consecration of virginity, which could take place only at age twenty-five. Solemn vows from adults were not accepted against their will.

In 789 Charlemagne restricted the power of abbesses to veil nuns, assigning this rite to the male clergy alone. Carolingian churchmen required that women religious choose either to live according to the Benedictine Rule or as noncloistered canonesses. Canons and canonesses retreated from life in the world, taking vows of chastity and dressing modestly in black or white. They lived according to the more flexible Rule of St. Augustine and were not required to give up their property. In the twelfth century, both male and female canons could be recognized by the white surplice, a cropped, wide-sleeved garment that was also part of the vestments of clergy, which they wore along with a black, blue, red, or gray habit.[20]

In 852 in Germany, the abbess of the monastery at Gandersheim required her nuns to dress alike and wear clothes "neither too rich nor too poor."[21] The Fourth Council of Constance (869–870) included the first universal legislation that required religious to wear a habit. Religious clothing, always an indicator of one's sacred purpose, became itself a sacred item. The cloth touched by saints—whether for clothing, funeral palls, or grave cloths—was divided and distributed as sacred relics after death. This was not a new idea. St. John Chrysostom (347–407) had written at an early date about the intrinsic value of such holy cloth: "How great is the power of saints. For the homage of Christians is directed not only to their words and bodies, but also to their vestments."

In spite of ecclesiastical legislation, many nuns continued to abide only by the customs of their abbey. One of the great medieval Benedictine abbesses, Hildegard of Bingen (1098–1197), depicted in her illuminated manuscript *The Garden of Delights* nuns of her convent dressed in secular aristocratic dress with brilliant red and purple veils. Her male contemporaries often chided Hildegard for her lavish taste in clothes, including the elaborate crowns she designed for her nuns from memories of her heavenly visions. She allowed her nuns to wear these ornaments along with loose, flowing hair and floor-length, luxurious white silk veils on feast days, reasoning that Christ should be presented with as much beauty as they could offer. Scholar Rebecca Sullivan believes that from this time forward, religious women developed a tradition of expressing imagination and inspiration through elaborately constructed headdresses. She believes the attention to precise folding, fluting, pleating, and draping emanated from the desire of nuns to represent themselves—regardless of male suggestions—through appearance. Some communities embroidered biblical mottoes along the edges of the veil and designed heavy, rigid coifs that would cause the veil to cascade around the head and body in precise patterns. Sullivan also suggests that nuns believed that the time and labor involved in creating these headpieces was in keeping with the honor and responsibility they felt went along with wearing them.[22] Clothing historian Desiree Koslin points out that the veil was a unique form of self-expression, and that orders' designs at times risked the disapproval of male clergy and others. Some nuns used ribbons and frills as decorative edging, attaching the veil by tucking it into a band of linen wrapped around the head and tied at the back of the neck, or secured to an underveil with decorative pins.[23]

At the same time, a new model of monastic community developed in France in the monastery at Cluny. Founded by the Duke of Aquitaine in 910, Cluny consolidated several Benedictine houses into one congregation, subject to one abbot who reported directly to the Holy See rather than to the local bishop. This organization sought to unify a common purpose and to revive the earliest spirit of Benedictine spirituality in areas where it had become lax. The movement centered on monks and had little immediate effect on women's communities.

The Cistercians, from 1098, took things further. As a reformed order of Cluniacs, they were much more rigorous. St. Thomas à Becket (1118–1170) resided at a Cistercian abbey and died wearing a knee-length hairshirt crawling with lice and worms.[24] At first, there were no female Cistercians, because the lifestyle was considered too difficult.

However, Cistercian nuns, called "White Ladies," eventually emerged. They followed a rule of silence and wore only rough, white woolen clothing, with the exception of a black veil for professed nuns. The nuns performed many of the same tasks as men, such as working in the fields and clearing forests. Beatrice of Nazareth (d. 1269) was a Cistercian prioress noted for her very severe austerities, such as wearing a girdle of thorns and compressing her body with cords.

The Benedictine way of life spread rapidly throughout Europe. Approximately a hundred new Benedictine communities were established in Germany alone between 1100 and 1199. In France, the famous abbess Héloïse (1100–1163) of the Order of the Paraclete wrote to her former lover, Abélard, that she could not live under the Benedictine Rule because it did not address women's specific needs. She mentioned as one example the impracticality of wearing woolen garments next to the skin while menstruating.[25] Although some Benedictine nuns wore a *camisia,* or undertunic, made from white linen or a mixture of wool and linen, it appears this practice was not universal.

Monasteries following the Benedictine Rule often added their own specific customs and regulations that addressed the particular characteristics of the community. In 1100 Robert d'Arbrissel (d. 1116) founded an order at Fontevrault in France, a double monastery with a female abbess. The rule at Fontevreault contained specific directives about clothing. It specified that the underveil and wimple should not be seen from beneath the veil, that the tunic be made from coarse undyed wool, that sleeve length not extend past the wrists, and that fringes and gloves not be permitted. Nuns observed continuous silence, abstained from meat, and wore veils that covered their faces.[26] At one time, between four and five thousand nuns were in residence there, most from noble families.

In 1131 Gilbert of Sempringham of England founded the Gilbertines, originally a group of hermit women who lived next to a church attended by poor village girls. These girls asked for a habit so that they too could live a religious life. By agreeing, Gilbert offered women of lower ranks the opportunity to participate in religious life and to become respected members of his community. Yet these sisters did not enjoy the full status of a nun. These "lay" sisters, a second class of nuns, were women with little education who would take on the menial tasks of the community.

In a drawing from the eighteenth-century work *Costumes of Religious Orders of the Middle Ages,* a Chartreuse nun is portrayed in her "ordinary habit of the house" as well as in her "choir habit," which includes the addition of a cape that almost completely covers her habit and opens in the front. When nuns chanted the Divine Office in choir—the area of the convent set aside for holy celebrations—or assisted at Mass, they typically dressed up in a finer habit or covered their everyday clothing with a choir cloak that came to be known under many names. Nuns of lay status did not wear these cloaks, as they did not participate in singing the Divine Office because of their lack of knowledge of Latin. This division then between choir and lay sister is one that would exist in some orders up until the 1960s. The Chartreuse nuns were unique in their maintaining of the ancient custom of solemn consecration of virgins, whereby the bishop invested them at their profession with a black veil as well as the stole and maniple (band of cloth worn on the arm), which were also clerical vestments. They wore the maniple on their right arm and the stole around their neck only on the day of their consecration and on the fiftieth anniversary of their profession.

Daily life in the convent consisted of cleaning, cooking, caring for clothes and altar cloths, copying manuscripts, and educating young students sent to them for instruction. Nuns also engaged in the manufacture of textiles and sewn items, ranging from fine embroideries, tapestries, and vestments to utilitarian cloth for religious habits and household uses. Nuns developed new technologies for cloth production and finishing. Although sisters provided hospitality to travelers, cared for the sick, and raised alms for the poor, their days centered on the internal rigorous schedules of fixed hours of prayer, vigils, and fasting. At times, early nuns petitioned for strict cloister so they could avoid the expense of providing room and board for friends, family, and clerical visitors. Yet monasteries and abbeys affected much of secular society around them, employing tradesmen and farmers, offering asylum or protection during political crises, and contributing beyond measure to the advancement of civilization through groundbreaking advancements in science, agriculture, medicine, philosophy, music, art, and literature. Modern history would be lost without the writings and records of the medieval abbeys and monasteries.

The purpose of female religious life at this time was to obtain graces through prayer and ascetic obedience. Monasticism also offered women prestige and a rare opportunity for an education, and many nuns became engaged in high levels of scholarship and the arts. Others entered convents to avoid the dangers of childbirth. If they were not suitable for marriage, due perhaps to a physical handicap, lack of a suitable wedding dowry, or dislike of an intended husband, or even for protection against violence, some women became "nuns" with no intention of ever professing vows. The English historian Eadmer (ca. 1064–ca. 1124) reported just such a situation involving Queen Margaret of Scotland's daughter Matilda:

> "I do not deny having worn the veil," the princess said. "When I was a child my Aunt Christina, whom you know to be a determined woman, in order to protect me against the violence of the Normans, put a piece of black cloth on my head, and when I removed it gave me blows and bad language. So I trembling and indignant wore the veil in her presence. But as soon as I could get out of her sight I snatched it off and trampled it underfoot."

Status Symbols

Because medieval nuns typically came from royal and noble ranks, they generally brought a handsome dowry to the convent upon acceptance, although the Church actually forbade the acceptance of this kind of fee. To get around the rules, nuns' families often donated lands, rental income, clothes, and furniture in lieu of cash. Popes tried again and again to regulate the clothing of monks and nuns, but most of their edicts were ignored. Instead, religious obeyed the dress regulations established by the general chapter (administrative body) of their order, or some simply followed their own personal tastes.

At this time in secular society, sumptuary legislation assigned specific furs to each social stratum. Although Pope Gregory IX (1145–1241) declared the skins of wild animals improper for any religious, monks and nuns often used them as a decorative lining in cloaks rather than employing the regulation lambskin. The Church history book, *Concilia Magnae Britanniae et Hiberniae,* cites other fancy items prohibited in medieval monk's costumes, presumably because they were being utilized, listing these items:

> ... ornamenting pendants, hoods with tippets of astonishing width, rings worn in public, costly girdles of marvelous magnitude, enameled and gilt purses with various images carved on them, knives worn at the side like swords, half-boots in red, checkered green cloth, shoes with pointed toes and cut in many ways, cruppers for the saddles, and horns hanging on necks, besides cloaks made of fur.

At this time, there were religious women who added only the veil to mark their monastic habit. Generally, a nun was chosen to oversee wardrobe requests and maintenance, but some communities distributed monies to individuals for purchasing clothing or permitted clothes to be accepted from friends and relatives. At the Benedictine monastery of St. Emmerman in Bavaria, a monk named Idung wrote a pamphlet attacking the nuns and monks he observed who did not wear monastic dress. He argued that although the Benedictine Rule did not necessarily ask nuns to cloister themselves, they should at least be obligated to use their clothing to identify their vocation.

Ideally, the dress of nuns of the medieval ages was to be some distinct religious version of the modest dress of the average married or widowed secular women of the time. Veils and wimples were part of this uniform. Eleventh-century Anglo-Saxon nuns kept their veil in place with a plain metal circlet, while secular women attached veils with half or complete circlets of gold. As abbess, eleventh-century Queen Gisela of Hungary wore her royal crown over her wimple and veil. Both nuns and laywomen also wore a fillet, a crownlike headpiece made from strips of linen. Young secular girls continued to wear their hair long and loose, while married women pulled theirs back under the veil.

The wimple came into secular fashion in the twelfth century, but continued to be worn by religious women for centuries afterward, and some sisters choose to wear wimples now. Secular women wore wimples of fine silk or linen in white in order to screen exposed areas of flesh. Wimples were long pieces of fabric that covered the neck and part of the chest and chin, the ends drawn up around the face and attaching at the top of the head. They evolved into complicated fluted or pleated affairs, requiring clamps, hot irons, and starch for their creation. Similar to the wimple, the barbette was a flat linen band that passed under the chin and was drawn up over the temples.

Gender Bending

In early Christianity, women seeking spiritual perfection were told to abandon their female nature, considered inferior to the male, and to "become men." The Council of Mâçon (585) even debated whether women had souls. St. Augustine and St. Ambrose lauded females who became "manly" in their beliefs, and St. John Chrysostom wrote of ascetic women who shaved their heads, wore chains around their necks, and dressed in sackcloth. Yet Church leaders made it clear that men's and women's clothing should remain distinct in some way, based both on strong social convention and Old Testament teaching (Deut. 22:5). St. Jerome advised his friend Eustochium to avoid women who wore men's clothes and thus "rejected nature."[27] The concept of maintaining gender differences in clothing has lingered on to the present day, which is why a man's shirt buttons on the right side and a woman's on the left.

Still, some women sought to achieve personal holiness through cladding themselves in men's clothing. In the sixth century Anastasia the Patrician donned male attire and lived as a monk to escape the romantic pursuit of the emperor Justinian (527–565) after the death of his wife, Empress Theodora. Castissima, a beautiful Alexandrian woman from the fourth or fifth century, shaved her hair and disguised herself in men's apparel to avoid marriage to her betrothed, hiding in a men's community to live out her dream of monastic life. Other women concealed themselves in male attire to conduct their lives undisturbed as hermits. The legends of these saints were very popular in medieval times, chronicled in such works as the *Old English Martyrology* (ca. 800) and Aelfric's *Lives of the Saints* (ca. 1000). Even Catherine of Siena (1347–1380) wrote that she had considered such a course of action until, as she described, Christ confirmed for her that a woman could praise God as well as a man.[28]

For the young St. Joan of Arc (1412–1431), adopting a male wardrobe had an altogether different outcome. Under command from God, Joan, known by her contemporaries as *la Pucelle* (the maid), gave up her female attire to lead the French army to victory in battle against the English and restore the crown of Charles VII. In spite of her remarkable accomplishments, Joan was imprisoned on charges of heresy, which included her *difformitate habitus* (unnatural clothing). She received no aid from her countrymen. Because her accusers were unable to make any of their charges hold fast, they bid her jailers to hide the female garb to which she had returned, leaving her former male clothing in its place. Joan had no choice but to resume wearing her battle dress to protect her modesty. In the end, she was convicted and burned at the stake because of a tricked confession, a fate perhaps hastened by her culturally challenging mode of dress.

A religious order for women was always connected to a male order or clerical supervisor who had agreed to take responsibility for the order's welfare. Theoretically, women's clothing had to meet with male approval, although this protocol was not always followed. However, in the Middle Ages, the Church began to enact universal legislation that would make local customs or community idiosyncrasies disappear. The Fourth Lateran Council (1215) reconfirmed the obligation for nuns and monks to wear the religious habit and placed the punishment of excommunication on those who did not. Episcopal regulations enacted at Fiesole, Italy, in 1306 stated that nuns who had permission to leave the convent could do so only in habit and could not change into secular dress.

The Church attempted to regulate clothing in secular society as well. The deep armholes of the medieval *surcote* were called *fenêtres d'enfer* (windows of hell), and the Gothic steeple-shape hennin (a tall, pointed hat) was regarded as a tool of the devil. Churchmen issued pamphlets on articles of clothing that were considered scandalous, such as the revealing, tight leggings worn by men called "plunderhose." Merchant-class women were expected to dress moderately, without "too much or too little frippery." Prostitutes, segregated at this time into "red light" districts, were prohibited from wearing ornaments or trimmings on their clothes, and offending articles were confiscated by authorities. Jews were forced to wear distinct symbols—for example, in some areas Jewish women were required to wear earrings during the fifteenth and sixteenth centuries, which were signs of social stigma. Governments and the Church used clothing as a means of control, and conformity maintained their power.[29]

CHAPTER FIVE

Emblem

$\mathcal{I}$n the Middle Ages, thousands of Christians lived in the Eastern
monasteries of Syria and Egypt and journeyed on pilgrimages to the
Holy Lands. Since the beginning of Christianity, there had been a constant exchange of ideas and artifacts across continents and cultures. As
a result, Eastern clothing had a great influence on Western costume—
the sleeves of the *dalmatic,* a garment worn by Christians still used as a
liturgical vestment today, were a Byzantine contribution, for example.
Arab turbans inspired similar styles of headdresses in the West, and it
became fashionable for Western ladies to wear the Muslim wimple that
concealed the lower part of the face. The upper ranks of society, particularly males, dressed brightly and lavishly—consider the priest's
elaborate vestments, the knight's armor, and the king's glamorous ensemble of colors and materials reserved for his exclusive use. When
travelers brought back foreign fabrics such as muslin, silk damask, and
fine cottons, European consumers eagerly purchased them. Yet by the
eleventh century, the Eastern empires had become a serious threat to
Christians at home and abroad. As a result, the crusaders set out to
protect and solidify the Christian empire.

Knights and Nurses

The name "crusades" relates to the word "cross," reflecting the emblem worn on the clothing of many of those who took part. Knights who pledged themselves to the service of God and Christendom formed chivalric orders that combined military life with religious vows, and from the start, women were associated with these communities of knightly ascetics. Established in 1190, the Teutonic Order accepted *consorores* (associated sisters) who assumed a female version of their habit and lived under the same rule. These sisters did not participate in the fighting but rather cared for the sick, occupying houses headed by a *commendatrix*, or prioress, in the same vicinity as their male comrades. Although they were not considered fully fledged knights, they sometimes wore half of the Teutonic Cross emblazoned on their clothing. The rule of the Knights Templars, a similar order, specifically prohibited the admission of more women in 1128, implying that they were at one time considered part of the organization. The Order of St. John was another organization that accepted female sisters for hospital work. Their habit was red with a black mantle, embroidered with the white Maltese cross. The Order of Santiago maintained convents late in the eleventh and thirteenth centuries, and records indicate that sixty-eight ladies were appointed to the Order of the Garter between 1358 and 1488 in England. These women wore the emblem of the garter on their left arm, as has been depicted on burial slabs from this time.

In 1198 St. John of Matha (1169–1213) and St. Felix of Valois (1127–1212) founded the Order of Trinitarians to redeem Christian captives who had become enslaved in foreign lands. Upon saying his first Mass as a diocesan French priest, St. John had a vision of Jesus seated on a throne with a slave on either side of Him. Christ appeared to be setting the slaves free. Around the same time St. Felix, a hermit from Cerfoid, France, beheld an apparition of the Blessed Mother dressed in what would become the Trinitarian habit: a white tunic and a white scapular that featured a large red-and-blue cross. According to legend, while having a conversation the two saints spotted a white deer in the forest, with a red-and-blue cross held between its antlers.

The order succeeded in procuring the release of thousands of captives. From the beginning of the thirteenth century, affiliate Trinitarian *sorores* dedicated their lives to worshipping the Trinity and assisting patients in the hospitals connected to their convents, living according to the Rule of St. Augustine. Presumably the nuns wore a habit similar to their male counterparts, with white symbolizing the purity of the Father, blue the humility of the Son, and red the sanctification of the Holy Spirit.

Medieval hospitals existed beyond those connected to the Crusades, however. Various male and female communities of hospitallers set up facilities to care for pilgrims and the general population of the sick, the elderly, and the poor. The most famous of these was the Hôtel-Dieu, established in Paris in 1097. Patients of early hospitals were subject to obeying the Benedictine or Augustinian rules of their caregivers and wore the religious habits of the order that nursed them. The Filles-Dieu of Orléans made their habit from a white tunic and a black mantle that featured the emblem of a red cross inside a white crescent moon. Religious women who worked in hospitals generally wore black, brown, or white habits.

Norbert of Xanten (ca. 1180–1134) founded the Prémontré Order initially to serve in hospices. They wore a coarse, undyed habit and a small black veil. The statutes for the order made provisions for various colors, however, based on local custom. The Premonstratensians, a group of canonesses, attracted so many women that Pope Innocent III forbade their acceptance of any more novices in 1198.

An order similar to the Premonstratensians originated in Sweden, known as the Brigittines. Founded by Birgitta (1303–1373), a Swedish princess and mystic, the order was established specifically for women. Birgitta reported that Christ had given her detailed instructions for their habit's design, including the distinctive four-cornered linen crown, which was decorated with five red circles to symbolize five drops of blood from Jesus' wounds. The Brigittine tunic and *cucullus* were fashioned from ash gray wool, with a fleece-lined mantle of the same fabric that fastened with a simple wooden button.[1]

Although many nuns were active in hospitals assisting their religious brothers, for the most part their lives remained hidden behind the convent walls. In the High Middle Ages (1000–1250), girls of low birth had the option of working in agriculture or in the textile industry to support themselves. However, religious life continued as the only career alternative to marriage for those of high birth. If a gentleman father had more daughters than he could fund sufficient dowries for, the convent presented a useful alternative. For women called to religious life, monasteries offered the ideal setting to become great writers, thinkers, and mystics. Yet convents also served simply as boarding-houses for secular females who had no other place to go. These fee-paying lodgers entered with no intention of becoming nuns and were free to leave whenever they chose. Nonreligious boarders often disturbed the monastic ideals of the convent by introducing colorful clothing, lapdogs, and other worldly distractions to the premises. Some religious sisters began to keep pet dogs, squirrels, rabbits, and birds, even taking the animals to church where they sat on elaborate jeweled and embroidered cushions while their mistresses recited their prayers. Chaucer describes the prioress Madame Eglentyne's "well-pinched wimple," elegant cloak, coral rosary, and gold brooch in his fourteenth-century *Canterbury Tales.* Bishops railed against nuns' finery, naming golden hairpins, silver belts, jeweled rings, laced shoes, brightly colored cloth, long trains, and furs in their complaints. Many religious sisters disapproved of frivolity too. A fifteenth-century English mystic had a vision of finely dressed comrades serving time in Purgatory wearing dresses made from painful hooks and headdresses from poisonous snakes.[2]

Male religious indulged in fine clothing as well. In 1283 legislation promulgated during the reign of Alfonso X of Castile, Spain, stated:

The King commands: that all of the clergy of his household be tonsured ... and that they may not wear bright red, green, or pink; that they may not wear stockings except of black, pale green, or dark brown; that they may not wear sendal [sandals], except for prelates and canons [who may use it] as lining; that they may not wear bright red or yellow tunics, shoes with strings, or closed detachable sleeves; that they must wear conservative clothing except for the prelates or the canon of the cathedral; and that they must use red or white saddles and bridles, except for prelates whose [saddles] may be red wool without other colors; that they may use breast leathers of silver except any that are suspended. ...

Pope Urban V (1310–1370) condemned the pontaine, the long-tipped male shoes of the fourteenth century, in which some religious men may have indulged. These were often fabricated in the shape of a beak, claw, or phallic symbol and were so long that they had to be reinforced by whalebone.

By the thirteenth century, large nunneries relied on secular servants to assist with the upkeep of their households. Because of an increase in nuns' leisure time, hours formerly spent on labor, prayer, and education began to used for dancing, drinking, dressing in costumes, and playing musical instruments. Besides the lax conditions in the monasteries, heretical teachings of groups like the Waldensians and Albigensians were taking hold in some areas of Europe. All of these factors set the stage for an era of reform.

Mendicants

As historians have wryly pointed out, quite a bit of money was required for religious orders to offer nuns a life of poverty. Monasteries had accumulated great wealth from patrons and bequests. However, a new type of monastic community emerged in the thirteenth century that rejected private ownership and all commonly owned property, considering extreme poverty an effective means to holiness. Distinct from the hermit or the cloistered monastic, the "mendicant" assumed extreme poverty in community in his or her pursuit of spiritual perfection. This new rigorous asceticism took inspiration from the words of Christ: "They should not put on two coats" (Mark 6:9). Just as the vow of chastity would cause any future marriage to be considered invalid, the vow of poverty prohibited the religious person from ownership irrevocably. Monks and nuns were called to support themselves entirely by begging alms or from their own labors. Nuns, for example, would tend sheep or manufacture textiles, but only enough to generate income for the barest level of substinance.

The mendicant, or "begging," movement began in Italy with St. Francis of Assisi (1181–1226). Opposing the wishes of his wealthy cloth merchant father, Francis sold his possessions and dressed in the coarse, neutral-colored garb of the peasant, adding a simple cord around his waist with three knots to represent the vows of chastity, poverty, and obedience. Brother Thomas of Celano (1200–1255) describes Francis's clothing in his *First Life of St. Francis of Assisi:* "He designed for himself a tunic that bore a likeness to the cross . . . a very poor and mean tunic, one that would not excite the covetousness of the world."[3] St. Francis wanted the garment to cost as little as possible and that it be mended with odd scraps of cloth when necessary rather than replacing the entire garment when it became worn. Art historian Cordelia Warr believes that the Franciscan habit was intended to make a very distinctive visual statement, and the tattered tunic, with its varied-colored patches, served as an unmistakable expression of extreme poverty. Francis's own garment has survived to this day and is on display in the Basilica of St. Francis, Assisi, Italy, a ragged and patched example of the poorest possible clothing a man might choose to wear.

St. Francis was concerned that the habit should reflect both the interior disposition of the friar and give a powerful exterior testimony of the monk's purpose. One popular Franciscan legend tells of the saint taking his companions into a town to preach. After they entered the village, they then turned around and left in silence. One of the brothers asked when the preaching was going to commence. Francis pointed to his habit and said that it already was complete. People flocked to Francis, and in 1209 he officially founded the Friars Minor. The brothers occupied their days with prayer and penance or with preaching about the love of Christ and begging for alms door to door. In 1210 Francis wrote a rule in which religious were asked to refrain from riding horses and from wearing shoes. Pope Innocent II approved the rule just a few years prior to the Fourth Lateran Council (1215), which banned the promulgation of any further formal rules.

A young noblewoman, Clare of Sciffi (1193–1253), had the opportunity to hear Francis preach in her town. She was so inspired that she set out to found a Franciscan order for women, and on Palm Sunday, March 19, 1212, Clare presented herself to Francis along with her plan. He responded by cutting her hair and clothing her in a sack bound with a cord. In spite of Clare's parents' protests, she stayed at a Benedictine convent, where she was quickly joined by her sister Agnes, until Francis could establish a proper facility for them. She became abbess of a convent at San Damiano, Assisi, in 1215 and later wrote her own austere rule for her nuns, who became known first as the Poor Ladies or Damianites, and later as Poor Clares. Pope Innocent IV approved the rule on her deathbed and issued a Papal Bull (official letter with affixed papal seal) declaring that Clare's nuns could never be forced against their will to break their vow of poverty. To date, this is the only example of a female religious order receiving the protection of the Holy See to pursue a lifestyle chosen by the community.

Poor Clares wore garments made from coarse wool that was "neither completely white nor completely black," a knotted cord belt, a black veil, and sandals without stockings. Their ensemble included a hairshirt, but Clare's rule allowed for variations:

Indeed, the abbess should rely on her own discretion regarding the aforementioned garments, taking into consideration the sorts of women, the places, seasons and cold climates of some regions, whatever may be dictated by need.

Italian Poor Clares employed a traditional custom at First Profession—when a postulant goes to change her clothes, a skeleton who represents "Sister Death" is moved forward by other sisters to embrace her.

Many female communities branched off from the Poor Clares to live as mendicants according to various interpretations and reforms. St. Francis also established a third order of Franciscans, so that lay husbands and wives might pursue the Franciscan way of life while remaining married. Called Tertiaries, they submitted to St. Francis's Third Order rule and wore a modified habit—a gray or brown tunic with a white cord with a hat or hood for men and a white veil for women. Those admitted followed a year's novitiate, professed limited vows, and adopted an ascetic lifestyle. Some interpreted the life of poverty more extremely—the beautiful St. Margaret of Cortona, a Franciscan Tertiary (1247–1297), was said to have once given all of her clothes to the poor, covering herself with a rush mat instead. Tertiaries enjoyed a high level of honor among their neighbors and were able to move about freely, greatly contributing to the conversion of their homelands. A remarkable number of illustrious women joined the Third Order throughout history, including the wife Louis IV of France, Queen Marie-Thérèse, who signed her name Soeur Thérèse and was buried in the Franciscan habit.[4]

Dominic of Osma (1172–1221) formed another of the great mendicant orders to combat the heresies of the Albigensian Cathars of France. When Dominic's mother was pregnant with him, she had a dream that she would bear a dog with a burning torch—this figure remains a part of the Dominican coat of arms. Dominic established a monastery for women at Prouille in 1206, because he learned that the gentry were sending their daughters to be educated at heretical Albigensian schools. He also believed that the success of his Order of Preachers would depend on the sisters' prayers of intercession. In establishing this community, he began a new partnership role for contemplative nuns, whom he considered vital participants rather than simply a "second" order. Like the Franciscans, there was also a Third Order. One famous Dominican tertiary was the mystic writer St. Catherine of Siena (1347–1380). This great saint committed herself to a life of celibacy at age seven, wearing a painfully coarse undershirt and iron chain even as a child.

Having previously lived under the Augustinian Rule, Dominic prescribed a rule for the nuns that followed Augustine's. He also stressed silence and recommended a habit of a white robe, brown mantle, and black veil. Later the nuns were given the official Dominican habit, which had been mystically bestowed on Reginald of Orleans (1183–1220) by the Blessed Virgin Mary on his sickbed. It included a white tunic, white scapular, black leather belt, and the striking black *cappa,* or mantle. Originally the black and white fabrics were undyed versions of the colors, so the hues varied from region to region. Unlike Franciscans, Dominicans wore shoes and socks. Superiors tried to enforce uniformity in the cut and color of shoes, but it often proved impossible. Commentary in the prologue of early Dominican constitutions states:

> Other orders also observe uniformity in their shoes. But with us one man has black shoes and another has red shoes; some wear coarse, religious shoes, while others wear worldly, open shoes. Some are fastened one way, some are fastened in quite another way. Some of us have got into the way of wearing shoes so large that they almost come up the knee, whereas others are very short, and some are in between.

The black *cappa* became the distinguishing feature of the Dominican habit and evolved into a ceremonial garment, like the *cucullus* of other orders, worn for solemn celebrations. Today Dominican nuns retain the custom of wearing the *cappa* at all liturgies and offices from Holy Thursday until the candlelight Easter Vigil Mass. As soon as the *Gloria* is intoned, the nuns dramatically remove their *cappas* to symbolize their joy in the Resurrection of Christ.[5]

The Carmelite order acquired mendicant status in 1247, but their history is much older and somewhat mysterious. In the mid-twelfth century, a group of pilgrims settled in the Holy Land on Mount Carmel to live an eremitic life reminiscent of the Old Testament prophets, filling their days with solitude, prayer, and contemplation. Yet records indicate that a monastery existed at Carmel as early as the fourth century, and some ancient writers claimed that the hermits of Carmel directly descended from converted Jewish Essenes, who originated as disciples of the prophet Elijah.

When the Carmelites relocated to the West, their seat was transferred to England with St. Simon Stock (1165–1265) as superior general. In 1251 Simon experienced a vision in which the Blessed Virgin Mary gave him what is now known as the brown scapular along with the promise that she would deliver its wearer from Purgatory the Saturday after his or her death. She spoke these words to him: "My beloved son, receive this habit of thy Order. This shall be to thee and to all Carmelites, a privilege that whosoever dies clothed in this, shall never suffer eternal fire." The promise later extended to all Christians who wore this emblem and practiced prescribed devotions. Today the brown scapular is worn under clothing as two small pieces of brown wool felt attached by a cord, hanging around the neck so that one square rests on the back and the other on the chest and neck, and it is worn at all times. Thus, when Pope John Paul II was shot in 1981, he told his doctors not to remove his brown scapular. The original Carmelite habit also included a boldly striped cloak, which is easily spotted in medieval art. Since stripes had a negative connotation in the West, as noted in the Council of Vienne in 1311, these cloaks became an object of ridicule. The Carmelites therefore exchanged their striped mantles for a white version.[6]

Around the time of the Protestant Reformation, St. Teresa of Ávila (1515–1582) established a small monastery in Spain that strove to return to the original ascetic Carmelite ideals, which had become lax over the years. She wrote a rule for her nuns that was fully dedicated to poverty, and her community became known as the Discalced Carmelite Order. The term "discalced," literally "without boots," would go on to indicate generally a reform branch of a religious order. In partnership with her friend St. John of the Cross (1542–1591), she extended her reform to men as well. In the beginning, the friars went barefoot, even in the snow, although Teresa did not approve of the practice. The nuns always wore *alpargatas*—sandals with leather tops and thickly plaited hemp soles, which they made themselves by pinning, sewing, and heating the material. Although some Carmelite nuns continue to wear the traditional footwear, many today wear a more comfortable leather sandal, chiefly because the old variety would be too time-consuming to produce in modern times. At first Teresa's nuns did not wear stockings or socks, but their history tells of an incident when the Venerable Anne of Jesus inadvertently displayed her bare ankle while climbing a mule cart. A passing driver expressed an admiring sentiment, so Teresa decided that her nuns' feet and limbs would be covered thereafter.

The habits of the Carmelite rule were originally made from old horsehair blankets, the poorest fabric available. St. Teresa was so revered that her Carmelite sisters focused their attention on every detail of her reforms. Madeleine of St. Joseph was the first French prioress of the Carmel founded in Paris in 1604. She was inflexible on the points that habits must be made only of the material chosen by St. Teresa and that all the forms and manners prescribed by the saint must be maintained. One day Madeleine learned that sisters had bought a bolt of fine wool serge with which to make habits. She was not at all satisfied and considered sending it back. Fearing that this would cause some loss to the seller, she reconsidered and ordered the material to be used for habits for the lay sisters, because they were involved in harder labor and their habits would wear out more quickly.

Mother Marianne Cope of Molokai (1838-1918): Partner of Blessed Fr. Damien, who worked with victims of leprosy on the island of Molokai, Hawaii. Though she wore the rough Franciscan habit of her community, Mother Marianne tailored beautiful clothing for her female patients to enhance their sense of optimism and self-worth. Her order is currently petitioning her cause for sainthood. *Courtesy of Archives of Mother Marianne, Sisters of St. Francis, Syracuse, New York*

Sisters of Bon Secours: Wearing the original habit, at left; and the first modification in 1960, at right. The Bon Secours were founded as a nursing order in France. *Courtesy of Sisters of Bon Secours USA Archives*

Maryknoll Sisters: In full habit with full-length capes in 1921. This order was formed specifically for foreign missionary work. *Courtesy of Maryknoll Sisters Photo Collection, Maryknoll Mission Archives, Maryknoll, New York*

Franciscan Sisters of Christian Charity: The sisters' habits featured a dramatic architectural headdress from 1869 to 1929. *Courtesy of the Archives, Holy Family Convent, Manitowoc, Wisconsin*

Franciscan Sisters of Christian Charity: The habit of sisters from 1929 to 1967. *Courtesy of the Archives, Holy Family Convent, Manitowoc, Wisconsin*

Franciscan Sisters of Christian Charity: Several new habit alternatives appeared after 1967. The sisters continue today to wear a veil and a modified white or black habit. A simple gold ring is worn by those who have made perpetual profession. *Courtesy of the Archives, Holy Family Convent, Manitowoc, Wisconsin*

Sisters of Providence: Sister John of God and Sister Jane Chantal visit with Chief Cholro and his companions at St. Ignatius, Montana, in the late 1800s. The French-Canadian sisters were among the first known white women to cross the Rocky Mountains, bringing previously nonexistent schools, hospitals, orphanages, and other institutions of care to the region.

Sisters of Providence: Getting ready for departure from Nome in 1918. The sisters were permitted to wear native-made parkas over their habits while traveling in the arctic climate of the Northwest.

Sisters of the Sacred Heart: Stationed in Honolulu, Hawaii, posing with parasols. They are wearing the original habit of the order, founded in 1797 in France. *Courtesy of Mr. Dan Paulos, St. Bernadette Institute of Sacred Art, Albuquerque, New Mexico*

Dominican Sisters, Queen of the Holy Rosary, 1961: The white monastic habit of these Dominicans varied little from that of the original order, founded in the 1200s. The uniformity of habits among sisters in the same community is well illustrated in this striking image. *Courtesy of Mr. Dan Paulos, St. Bernadette Institute of Sacred Art, Albuquerque, New Mexico*

Japanese Poor Clare Sister: Some Poor Clare nuns continue the tradition of shearing their hair at profession and placing it in a basket overnight with a blessed crucifix. The Poor Clares were founded by Saint Clare (1194–1253), in Assisi, Italy. *Courtesy of Mr. Dan Paulos, St. Bernadette Institute of Sacred Art, Albuquerque, New Mexico*

Sisters of Charity of Seton Hill: The habit of the American Sisters of Charity was based on the "widow's weeds" worn by their foundress, St. Elizabeth Seton, the first native-born U.S. citizen to be canonized. Mother Seton's sisters cared for wounded soldiers in the American Civil War at the request of Abraham Lincoln. *Courtesy of Mr. Dan Paulos, St. Bernadette Institute of Sacred Art, Albuquerque, New Mexico*

Sisters of Charity: Sisters of Charity of New York participate in a civil rights march in Harlem, 1965. Their habit makes a bold statement, remaining unchanged from the previous century. *Courtesy of Mr. Dan Paulos, St. Bernadette Institute of Sacred Art, Albuquerque, New Mexico*

Passionist Nuns: Religious from the community established at St. Gabriel's Monastery in Scranton, Pennsylvania, 1926. Founded in Italy in 1770, the Passionists wore an all-black habit featuring their distinct heart-shaped emblem. *Courtesy of Mr. Dan Paulos, St. Bernadette Institute of Sacred Art, Albuquerque, New Mexico*

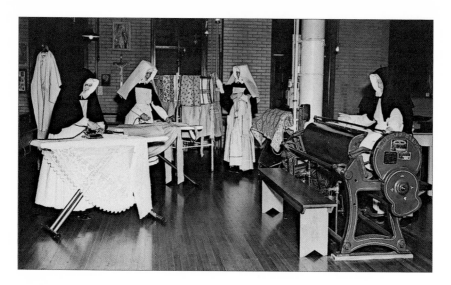

Sisters of Christian Charity: Engaged in the complicated process required for the maintenance of their habits at the Illinois motherhouse laundry in 1949. This order was founded in Germany a century earlier. *Courtesy of Mr. Dan Paulos, St. Bernadette Institute of Sacred Art, Albuquerque, New Mexico*

School Sister of St. Francis Clare Korte is currently a professor of biology at Saint Mary's University of Minnesota in Winona. Many sisters today choose to dress in clothing specific to their work. When not working in the lab, Sr. Clare typically wears a skirt and blouse, along with a Tau Cross pin or pendant, which is the symbol of her community. *Courtesy of the School Sisters of St. Francis U.S. Province Communications Office, Milwaukee, Wisconsin*

The Carmelites were the first female order to arrive in the United States, settling in Port Tobacco, Maryland, in 1790. St. Teresa of Ávila, a brilliant writer and visionary, went on to become the first female Doctor of the Church, an honor bestowed on her in 1970 by Pope Paul VI. Another Carmelite received this honor in 2000 and is one of the most beloved saints in modern day—St. Thérèse of Lisieux (1873–1897), "the Little Flower." She remains a familiar nineteenth-century image of one who wore the Carmelite habit.

Enclosure

The mendicants' lifestyle varied greatly for religious men and women of the same order. While friars ventured out beyond the confines of the monastery to engage in preaching and evangelical missionary work, their female counterparts remained bound to the convent. The brothers mingled with the people, teaching them popular acts of devotions, such as the Rosary, in their own languages. The nuns focused on uniting themselves to God through mystical experiences and reciting the Latin prayers of office in choir. It had always been the practice for women religious to remain enclosed in the East, but Western sisters often had interpreted the concept of cloister differently, interacting with secular society in various capacities. In 1283 Pope Boniface VIII (1235–1303) incorporated permanent cloister as a part of canon law, mandating that all professed nuns live in perpetual enclosure. He imposed this regulation both as a protection for women against brutal barbarian invasions and as a means of completely separating the religious from worldliness. However, this regulation prevented women from performing charitable works for the laity and greatly inhibited their ability to make a living. As with clothing regulations, it is impossible to know to what extent the regulation was enforced. Historian Will Durant points out that Chaucer's prioress in *The Canterbury Tales* would not have been permitted to be on pilgrimage, had she been obeying the laws of the times.[7] Art historians also surmise that because so many secular paintings feature nuns, they must have been able to interact with the outside world at times. Furthermore, the Black Death of the mid-fourteenth century claimed the lives of large numbers of religious who cared for the sick, presumably including those outside the convent walls, as so many died from the plague.

Some women preferred to live the enclosed life alone, rather than in community. These hermit religious were known as anchoresses—consecrated virgins who were given episcopal permission to be enclosed in a small cell. Their housing typically existed near or attached to a church, so they could meditate on the Blessed Sacrament housed there. A lady in waiting passed their meals through a small window and attended to their other various needs. Sometimes several anchoresses had cells joined together under one roof. Anchoresses spent their days in prayer or light labor, such as needlework or spinning. Some cells were so small that the occupants could barely move around. Many anchoresses followed the Ancrene Riwle, a set of guidelines believed to have been written by Simon of Gent, Bishop of Salisbury (1297–1315) for three solitary ladies. It prescribed a code of behavior, including direction on dress: "The garments should be of such a shape, and all their attire such that it may be easily seen to what life they are dedicated. . . ." In place of a religious habit, the Ancrene Riwle advised "Keeping oneself unspotted from this world . . . in this lies religion: not in the wide hood or a black cape, nor in a white rochet or a grey cowl."

Other women who wished for the life of poverty and religious service outside the confines of cloister banded together from the thirteenth century in Europe to form loose communities known as Beguinages. The Beguines were often skilled textile experts who supported themselves independently from monastic affiliations. Some took simple vows before the village priest; these could be renewed periodically but were not perpetually binding like solemn vows, which could be dispensed only for the gravest of reasons and then only by the pope himself. Although they distinguished themselves with a veil, the Beguines were not considered true religious. They wore simple beige or black clothing, and some groups had clothing regulations imposed on them by clerical authorities. The Bishop of Langres (1239–1260) composed a rule for Beguines that called for the woolen cloth used for tunics to be made from wool spun from three-quarters white wool and one-quarter black fibers.[8] Any luxuries in dress, which the Beguines probably would not have been able to afford in any event due to their wish for poverty, were forbidden.

The Holy Habit

The religious habit became so highly esteemed that it was all but worshipped. The lay mystic Margery Kempe (ca. 1373–ca. 1440), who wrote the first known autobiography in the English language, tried to persuade her bishop to allow her to wear the religious habit, even though she was not a religious. Here is an except from the exchange:

> My Lord, if you please, I am urged from within my soul that you should clothe me with the mantle and the ring and that you should clothe me overall in white. For I have learned by a revelation that if you clothe me like this on earth, our Lord will clothe you in heaven.

The *Lay Folks' Catechism* of 1357 instructed readers that a habitual sinner could not gain entrance to heaven simply by wearing the Holy Habit.[9] In 1256 Bishop Eudes of Rouen threatened to deprive a group of nuns of their veils because of problems he had observed while visiting their convent. He also tried to force them to adopt a uniform habit, even though they were impoverished and had to rely on clothing gifts from friends.[10] Both males and females agreed that uniformity was one way to suppress individual desires and encourage common spirit, although it appears that the authors of rules for women tended to focus on clothing in a more rigid manner than authors of rules for men.

In the High Middle Ages, the habit stopped following the trends in clothing among general society and solidified into forms that would carry on for centuries and to present times in some cases. The veil and wimple combination, for example, was abandoned by secular ladies for hairnets, fluted face ruffles, and horned-shaped hats with veils used only for decoration. Nuns and widows continued wearing loose-fitting tunics, while gentle female society moved to fitted, laced gowns that revealed the breasts. Color became a distinguishing factor for various orders—communities were known as the Gray Sisters or the White Ladies. Because the Church forbade new religious rules, the habit became one of the most important emblems of a community. And as the need to differentiate increased as numbers of communities grew, the habit began to become stylized and even extravagant in some cases. The habit became a precise collection of forms and emblems that would continue to represent religious life until modern times.

Charity

$\mathcal{A}$t the same time that the Fifth Lateran Council (1512–1517) decreed that the religious habit was a deterrent to worldliness, material-
ism, and moral decay, a radical new theology began its sweep across
Europe. An Augustinian monk named Martin Luther (1483–1546)
launched the Protestant Reformation in 1517 by pinning his Ninety-
five Theses to a church door at Wittenberg University. It spread like
wildfire, and Luther's challenges to Catholicism would result in significant devastation. The mendicant orders that had prospered in the fifteenth century drastically declined. Convents were forced open and
vandalized. Iconoclasts shattered stained glass, painted over artworks,
and stole the clappers from chapel bells. Many of the great monasteries of England, Scotland, Ireland, Holland, and Scandinavia disappeared completely.

The reformers focused especially on religious habits, ripping them
to shreds or burning them, ordering sisters to adopt secular dress. Some
nuns refused; others wore their habits secretly under their imposed lay
attire, as it was recorded of religious in Augsburg. Walled convents were
ordered to install windows to bring the inhabitants into public view.
Protestants proclaimed the idea of celibacy as unnatural, declaring
marriage to be the most illustrious state and therefore seeking to "lib-
erate" nuns so they could be free to marry. Reformation intellectual
Desiderius Erasmus (1466–1536) penned satirical tales about convent

life that became extremely popular with the general public. In England, King Henry VIII closed monasteries and obliterated orders in order to gain their lands. Later Oliver Cromwell (1599–1658) and his Puritan Roundheads escalated Catholic persecution with fierce brutality—his army slaughtered over 40 percent of indigenous Irishmen, for example, who clung to their faith. Rather than being an agent of reform, the Protestant movement became a tyrannical suppression of religious freedoms of non-Protestants.

The Council of Trent convened in 1545 to reunify the devastated Catholic Church. The Council established a strict new code by which nuns were to live and promulgated enclosure for all nuns under pain of excommunication. All consecrated women living in community were required to take solemn vows and live in cloister. Abbesses could no longer leave the convent to participate in the politics of their countries. The rules of enclosure became enforced to an extreme degree; even in the nineteenth century, when an English community of Carmelites traveled to another town to start a new community, they rode in a coach with the windows painted black.[1] The religious habit also received great attention from the Council, which saw it as a means to assist the renewal of religious life. Trent banned the secular dress that some nuns had taken up as a result of political unrest. It focused on uniformity in dress and made it part of Church law that the habit was to be given at the beginning of a sister's novitiate.

This strict legislation fostered an entirely new mode of religious life. New orders began to establish themselves purposely outside of the boundaries that Trent had set up. These orders did not accept solemn vows or the religious habit and created a way of life intended precisely to avoid the restrictions of cloister, so that the sisters could interact with the public and practice works of charity. These new groups wanted to establish a clear break with the religious of former times. The Church, however, did not recognize these apostolic communities or individuals as true religious.

A New Kind of Habit

In 1536 St. Angela Merici (1474–1540) founded such an organization in Italy, known as the Ursulines. She obtained permission from her diocese to write a nonmonastic rule for women that required no public vows, common residence, or monastic clothing. Angela, a Franciscan tertiary, desired that the sisters should live at home with their parents and perform all manner of charitable works out in the world, from teaching children to working with the sick in hospitals. Angela's successor, Lucrezia Lodrone, created a habit for Italian sisters that caused problems when unauthorized women adopted the same clothing but not the same pious lifestyle. It consisted of a black dress, white linen collar, black veil, black belt, and black footwear. Ursulines in France elected to wear a more traditional habit, and as an international organization, they adopted a uniform in 1928 that combined "the cincture of Paris, the ring of Italy, the headdress of America, the wimple of Angers, the crucifix of Toulouse and the veil of Bordeaux."

It was not until St. Ignatius of Loyola (1491–1556) founded his Society of Jesus, however, that religious life truly transitioned into a new era. In 1540 St. Ignatius introduced a new type of religious community dedicated to missions and education. The Jesuits wore regular clerical clothing rather than religious habits. They professed simple vows prior to professing solemn vows, a new practice that eventually would be adopted by all modern orders. In 1616, Englishwoman Mary Ward set out to emulate this new example and petitioned the pope to found a society of teaching nuns. Like the Jesuits, her sisters would answer to a superior general who was directly responsible to the Holy See. Ward proposed to create a lifestyle that would emulate the one lived by the Blessed Virgin Mary after the death of Christ. Pope Paul V (1550–1621) gave his approval for the group, called the English Ladies but informally nicknamed the "galloping girls."[2] Ward instituted a simple black dress with a white linen collar, simple white cap, and transparent black veil. The idea of noncloistered nuns was very unpopular, however. Church officials later tried to impose cloister on the institute, and because Mary Ward refused to comply, the institute was suppressed in 1631.

In 1610 the widowed Baroness Jeanne de Chantal and Francis de Sales (1567–1622) founded the Order of Visitation in France to visit the sick and poor. They dressed simply in a black dress and veil without ornamentation. Townspeople were so offended by seeing them out on their rounds, out of the confines of cloister, that they insulted the sisters and spat on them.[3] As a result, the Archbishop of Lyons believed that the order should abandon its cause. Eventually St. Francis unhappily accepted the restrictions of cloister so that the community might survive. The Visitation nuns became a haven for widows and girls with physical disabilities, individuals who would not have been accepted into religious orders of the time.[4]

Social conditions were deplorable in mid-seventeenth-century France. Major famines and fever epidemics resulted in over forty thousand homeless people in Paris alone. No public assistance existed at this time, and there was a great need for people to help. Almost immediately after the Visitation nuns adopted enclosure, Henri de Maupas, Bishop of Puy, tried to accomplish St. Francis de Sales's original goal. In 1650 he approved the founding of a noncloistered order, the Sisters of St. Joseph, founded by the Jesuit missionary Jean-Pierre Medaille to serve the sick and poor of his area. Father Medaille asked the sisters to dress in a habit similar to the costume of widows of the day so that they could walk the streets without suspicion. One historian recalled the following anecdote:

> In the city of LePuy, people soon began to know and to venerate these modest and dignified sisters who went quietly about the streets. They resembled humble widows in their black dress. Around their shoulders they wore a simple linen kerchief that crossed in front. Suspended from the neck hung a bronze

crucifix. When they went out into the streets, they wore their taffeta coif.

Their founder intended that they would practice "all the spiritual and corporal works of mercy of which women are capable." Their clothing was meant to adapt to their particular social situations, and there were differences in the dress of nuns in the countryside and the city. They wore a crucifix and Rosary, yet the dress was designed to be neither uniform nor to resemble that of religious orders of the day.

The widow's costume was one that was very recognizable to society of the times, firmly established by the fifteenth century. In Egypt mourners wore yellow as a symbol of withered leaves. In Ethiopia they wore gray for the color of ashes, and in Rome white or violet was worn, symbolizing purity. Mourning clothing was more strictly observed by women than by men. Wives and daughters followed various customs of shrouding themselves or their rooms when in mourning, usually for a period of one year. By the 1300s black was recognized in northern Europe as the symbolic color of grief. Medieval mourners wore a dark-colored garment with an enveloping hood, sometimes called the *cappa*, over their normal clothes. Victorian mourning customs became extremely elaborate, with widows covered head to foot in black fabric, including gloves and handkerchiefs, their faces screened with heavy black veiling. By degrees over time, they replaced black clothing with colors of white, lavender, and gray.

In 1633 St. Vincent de Paul (1580–1660) and St. Louise de Marillac (1591–1660) founded the Daughters of Charity in France to nurse the sick of the Hôtel-Dieu and to serve the "poorest of the poor." They also raised funds to "purchase" orphan children, saving them from the cruel conditions of the public asylums, and to establish *potageries économiques* (early soup kitchens). Their constitution notes:

> . . . having no monastery but the houses of the sick and the place where their superior lives, having no cell but a rented

room, no chapel but the parish church, no cloister but the streets of the city, and no enclosure but obedience, they should go to the sick and to other places when it is necessary for their service having the fear of God for a grille and holy modesty for a veil.

The Daughters of Charity made simple vows and adopted the country dress of the peasant women of the Île de France, something that many of the more educated and high-ranking sisters did not initially applaud. St. Vincent believed that this costume, based on simplicity, would make the women more approachable by the poor, and because they would not be recognized as religious women, their non-cloistered status would not present a problem.

Their dress was of uniform design, because the founder wanted to ensure equality within the ranks. Prior to its adoption, some sisters who did not live in the motherhouse had added little extras to their dresses, veils, and capes. The first sisters wore a gray wool serge dress, a white collar, and a white linen kerchief wrapped closely around their heads. This head covering provided very little protection from the damp and cold climate; the sisters pointed out that peasant women wore some kind of bonnet and asked if they could wear the same. St. Vincent agreed but mandated that it be a standard design. The sisters then began to wear the famous white cornette that would become a beloved and universally recognized symbol. By 1685 the cornette became obligatory, but it was not until 1750 that the hat took on starched, folded "wings." The cornette acted as a symbolic protection and shelter, representing white walls and calm corridors and giving a sense of privacy and reserve. The center point directed eyes to heaven.

The sisters became known by their hats as God's Geese or Heaven's Seagulls; in the mission territories, Muslim hospital patients referred to the sisters reverently as "the swallows of Allah." The hats became a poetic trademark of their religious service. When General Charles de Gaulle was informed that the Sisters of Charity were changing their head covering in the 1960s to a soft veil, he said, "What? Changing the cornette of the Sisters of Charity? Well, one might as well propose changing the French flag!"[5]

The New World

While new communities of sisters adopted simple lifestyles and focused on working with the poor, the older, established orders maintained their traditional way of life. They also established branches in foreign lands. Nuns in the New World added their own twist to the dress codes of the motherhouses back in Europe. Some South American sisters stitched dazzling ornaments to their habits and used colorful fabrics in their design. In Mexico from the 1630s to the nineteenth century, it was the custom in many orders for nuns to wear elaborately painted badges as part of their habit. Worn in the same position as one would wear a cross, these badges often functioned as clasps for mantles, and some included a metal loop or pin. They were fashioned from copper, tortoiseshell, or finely inlaid wood and could be surprisingly large. The *escados de monja* (nun's badges) featured meticulously executed images of the Blessed Virgin Mary with or without Christ, sometimes surrounded by the patron or favorite saints of the nun.[6]

According to historian Kathryn Burns, the nuns of Cuzco, Peru, used the veil to maintain the rigid social hierarchy so important to the times. Although authorities insisted that all professed nuns wore the same habit and veil, the founder of the convent at Santa Clara used the *velo negro* (black veil) and the *velo bianco* (white veil) to create a new class of sisterhood, something between the professed nun and the lay sister. The white veil meant that the sister paid only half of the unofficial required dowry. As a result, she received a smaller food ration and was not allowed to vote in convent elections.[7]

Class consciousness remained extremely strong in both secular and religious circles for centuries to come. In 1753 Louis XV of France appointed the widow Madame Marguerite d'Youville as directress of the General Hospital of Montreal, establishing a new institute of the Sisters of Charity, who would become known as Grey Nuns. Although the community received full civil and ecclesiastical approval, many in Montreal did not look kindly on it. The idea of gentlewomen performing works of charity for persons beneath them in social standing remained a radical notion. Even Marguerite's own relatives and friends frowned on her activities. The townspeople mocked and ridiculed the sisters, sometimes going so far as to pelt them with stones on their way to church. The women were falsely accused of selling liquor to the Indians and even of becoming intoxicated themselves, earning them the name *Les Soeurs Grises,* which in French means "The Tipsy Nuns." A few years later, Marguerite designed a distinctive habit for the community made from gray woolen fabric, but not without a bit of sardonic humor, because in French, *grise* also means the color gray.[8] To this simple gray uniform, she added a black headdress similar to that which was worn by widows of the time. She added a silver cross embossed with a heart at its center and a fleur-de-lis at each corner, to commemorate the sisters' French origin.

Revolution

Back in Europe, some of the new teaching sisters of the seventeenth century wore rich clothing in deference to their social status and that of their clientele, whom they imagined would be put off by the mendicant styles of the past. In some orders, poverty was no longer stressed. When the distinguished mystic Marguerite d'Arbrouze accepted the position of abbess of the convent at Val de Grace, she found the nuns there dressed in beautiful gowns and adorned with jewels. Women continued to rent rooms at convents, entertaining friends and conducting business there. When a famous opera star took up residence in a convent, the sisters allowed her to perform for friends and fans.[9]

Clothing in secular society continued to be regulated with sumptuary legislation. The sixteenth-century Peasant's Revolt in Germany carried demands that those in lower levels of society be permitted to wear red. The English Parliament in 1571 required apprentices to wear a flat hat. In France the rich favored powdered wigs and beauty spots. Clothes became rigid, fashioned with underlying framework, board, or stiffeners that made them so difficult to negotiate that people could dress only with the help of servants. Underwear went from a layer for warmth and protection to serve as a body-contouring foundation for outer garments. Styles for servants and lowborn persons lagged behind the fashions of the rich and retained forms from earlier eras, such as the close-fitting coif head covering. Married women continued to cover their heads, utilizing turbans, beehive-shape hats, mantillas, and linen caps with long side lappets, serving mostly as a decorative token rather than as an indication of marital status.

The extravagant fashions of the rich incensed many in the poorer levels of society, giving a visible reminder of the differences in wealth. Marie Antoinette (1755–1793), Queen of France, spent the modern-day equivalent of about $700,000 on clothes in 1785. Even when she was taken captive, Marie ordered new clothes and billed the New Republic of France in 1791. Revolutionaries sought to equalize clothing between the classes—*"sans cravates"* was one battle cry, meaning "no more neckties." Dress was a powerful tool in the French Revolution. Revolutionaries created a standard of uniform that resembled that of the working person and adopted a distinctive red hat as a badge of freedom. Although many aristocrats abandoned their fancy clothing, some chose to wear a black velvet collar after the execution of Louis XVI as a sign of mourning for their monarch. Those who sided with the royalists took up the symbols of the Sacred Heart of Jesus and the Rosary to demonstrate their loyalties—in Brittany, nuns were arrested for embroidering the Sacred Heart emblem. A Carmelite community was charged for possessing altar cloths decorated with symbols honoring the royal family, such as the fleur-de-lis.[10]

By 1770 there were approximately 300,000 religious worldwide. At this time, the penal laws remained in force against Catholics in Ireland, subjecting to harassment those who wished to educate their children. Yet Honora "Nano" Nagle (1718–1784) established the Sisters of the Presentation to teach the Catholic children in her native city of Cork. Nano and her sisters operated in secret, fashioning a habit from a black gown, a black silk handkerchief crossed in front, and a plain black cap that fit closely to the head and fastened with a broad black ribbon. Their dress was modeled after the Ursulines, whom Nano hoped to recruit to work with her; because the Ursulines maintained the rule of enclosure, however, they were not able to participate in her traveling apostolate. Nano's sisters wore the habit only on feast days and for ceremonial purposes, donning a long, hooded cloak if they needed to go out in public.[11]

In France, nuns—especially contemplative ones—were thought by the revolutionaries to lead useless, frivolous lives. Deeply connected to the aristocracy, Catholic clergy and religious were a key target of the revolution in France. The Age of Enlightenment pitted man against religion, and the Revolution's Reign of Terror (1793–1794) committed itself to secularizing society. In 1789 religious communities were ordered to disband. Nuns were offered the choice of leaving their convents with a state pension or remaining behind to face the angry mobs. Those who would not agree to the new terms were convicted of "fanaticism." Many religious orders split apart but continued their way of life underground in clandestine small groups. The revolutionary government prohibited the wearing of a religious habit and professing new vows. In October 1791 the nuns at an English convent in Rouen were forced to remove their habits in exchange for street clothing, and their home was turned into a prison. One nun recorded:

> ... It was a very severe slavery at that time whilst we had the cruel task of changing our dress. It is not easy to conceive of what a piece of work it was to clothe 42 people from head to

toe, especially as we had neither wherewithal to make clothes nor money to buy them. We were obliged to cut up the curtains of eleven beds and many large window curtains to make gowns but these were far from supplying our necessities; the lady prisoners and other benefactors in the town were very charitable in giving us money, cottons and stuffs, otherwise we could never have compassed our task. We were obliged to work night and day for we were continually threatened with a more severe prison if we did not put off our religious habits.[12]

In 1792 the Ursulines at Valenciennes were sent to the guillotine after they tried to escape. Nuns were imprisoned in foul conditions and executed. Marie de l'Incarnation wrote of her Carmelite sisters who pieced together enough of a habit to wear it to the guillotine, having cut the wimples to prevent the executioners from touching them. As each nun climbed the scaffold, she asked permission to ascend and renewed her vows before her superior. One sister declared, "We are the victims of this age and we should sacrifice ourselves for its reconciliation with God."[13]

In 1794 the French Revolution advanced to Belgium. The governor of Brussels warned a group of Benedictine nuns to leave the city. Within twenty-four hours, the sisters replaced their habits with whatever garments they could find—one nun made a shawl from a tablecloth, while others donned fur-lined cloaks even though it was midsummer. The abbess stayed behind, refusing to accompany her sisters to Holland. English Benedictines stationed on the continent also faced imprisonment and death. After the Revolution, the number of Benedictine communities in Europe declined from approximately two thousand to just twenty.

At this time, the Holy See declined to approve the creation of any new communities that required solemn vows, because political unrest made it more and more difficult for religious women to maintain them. The Church abolished new professions in the older orders in Belgium and France. Henceforth nuns were formally separated into two divisions: those with solemn vows, who answered directly to Rome, and those accepting only simple vows, who were under the jurisdiction of the local bishop.

Sisters continued to form new communities with simple vows in order to perform charitable work. In 1797 Marie Anne Rivier founded the Sisters of the Presentation of Mary in France; they wore poor, coarse garments and committed themselves to teaching religion to the children and adult women of the displaced parishes. After the Daughters of Charity lost sixteen sisters to the guillotine, they adopted street clothes for a short time but returned to their habit quickly. Napoleon admired the sisters and decreed, in 1809, "The Sisters of Charity shall continue to wear their present costume." He recognized the great social service provided by the nuns and supported such congregations with state funds and property, although he did not do so with contemplative orders.[14]

The Age of Reason rejected the legitimacy of religious life, placing a veneration for science over trust in religion. In an era of extreme persecution, many nuns remained joined together by a common purpose rather than a common habit. It was indeed a dark period for the Roman Catholic Church. During the Terror, tens of thousands of Catholics were persecuted or killed, and scores of religious were scattered across Europe. As a result, many nuns looked to America for a new start.

CHAPTER SEVEN

Courage

After the turmoil of the French Revolution, many orders and congregations regrouped and even expanded. Hundreds of new communities formed in the nineteenth century. The habit served as a rallying point, binding the new communities together, but due to the sheer numbers of new orders, visually distinguishing one group from another became more and more difficult. To gain Church approval for a new design, a community's habit had to appear sufficiently different from those of existing orders. Mother Mary Euphrasia founded the Sisters of the Good Shepherd in France in 1835 and based their white habit on that of the Sisters of Our Lady of Mary, of which she had formerly been a member. However, the Holy See mandated that some recognizable changes be instituted, so she altered the design of the silver heart pendant and added a blue waist cord with tassels. Likewise, the Sisters of Providence, who started out with a gray habit, later adopted a black habit to set themselves apart from the Grey Nuns.

Nuns used elaborate folding, variety in color, and distinct emblems to accomplish this differentiation and as a result paid great attention to the smallest details of the costume. The length of a belt, for example, became precisely regulated. Often elements of the habit originated due to mere chance. One modern Dominican sister recalls that when a branch of the community split off to found a house in a new area, the sisters asked for a habit to be sent to them at their new location. When it arrived, the headband featured a distinct crease from being folded in the shipping box. Thinking it part of the design, the new group retained the crease from then on. The Sisters of Christian Charity first received their habits in Germany in 1849. After the ceremony, the brother of their foundress, Blessed Pauline von Mallinckrodt, playfully tapped his cane on the center of his sister's head, causing her white coif to dip in the center and resemble a heart shape around her face. The other sisters liked the idea so much that it was adopted into the design permanently.[1]

The Sisters of Notre Dame wore the peasant dress of their foundress. The black serge garment featured a gathered skirt and crossover bodice fastened with a large steel pin. Later, when it would have been safer and easier to use snaps, the sisters could not adapt this closure because the pin had been specified in their rule. The Society of the Sacred Heart, founded in the aftermath of the French Revolution, used silver-engraved buttons in their habit designed by their foundress, St. Madeline Sophie Barat (1719–1865). As the years went by, the buttons became an enormous expense, completely incongruous with the plain widow's costume the saint chose to be "simple and common to all."

The new apostolic congregations preferred to adopt either the dignified dress of the widows of the day or the plain, country garb of the poor. Whatever the design, religious habits moved in the direction of becoming more uniform and standardized, and some became quite stylized and elaborate. Great attention continued to be placed on the pieces worn around the head and neck. In mid-nineteenth-century England, the Sisters of the Cross of Passion wore a straw bonnet with voluminous black veiling that drew so much attention that they had to abandon it.[2] Some orders adopted bonnets or caps framed by a pleated frill. A frill that fit around the face might start as a piece of fabric as long as the length of a room, requiring hand hemming and processing through a goffering machine. Each frill could take up to ninety minutes to starch and pleat—thus, the idea of the habit being simple and inexpensive to produce fell by the wayside.

Nuns in America

Nuns moved to the United States to serve the immigrant Catholics who had relocated there. They first arrived from France, Canada, Germany, and Ireland. Later Italian and Polish sisters embarked for American shores. Between 1809 and 1891 more than two dozen communities formed within the United States to establish schools, particularly to assist with educating children in their new language and to care for the poor and sick. The first American to be canonized, Mother Frances Xavier Cabrini (1850–1917), between 1889 and 1917 established sixty-seven schools, hospitals, and orphanages across the country at the request of Pope Leo XIII (1810–1903). Other orders of sisters committed to helping newly emancipated African American slaves and Native American populations.

Although some communities tried to maintain their European way of life, often the climate in America was unsuitable. The founder of a group of Sisters of Loretto in Kentucky required nuns to go barefoot, sleep on the floor, labor in the fields, and clear land. The Kentucky winter was so different from the temperate European climate to which they were accustomed that, in one year, fifteen of sixteen sisters under the age of thirty perished from tuberculosis.[3]

The biggest obstacles for sisters came from American attitudes toward Catholics. Borrowing the ideals of the French Revolution, the democratic society in America was suspicious of those who pledged allegiance to Rome. Although John Carroll (1735–1815), the first American Catholic bishop, strove to establish an assimilated, Americanized version of Catholicism, a rift existed from the start, as many orders clung to their old-world customs and traditions. Catholics formed their own school systems, parishes, and for a long time remained segregated in their own province of Maryland. Samuel Morse, the inventor of the telegraph, wrote a series of articles against the "foreign conspiracy" of Catholic communities in Ohio. Anti-Catholic secret societies and social organizations like the Ku Klux Klan, the Know-Nothing party, and the American Protective Association rallied against Catholic "antipatriotic popery." Abraham Lincoln wrote in 1856, "If the Know-Nothings get control, the Declaration of Independence will read: All men are created equal except for Negroes, foreigners, and Catholics."[4]

Because of their singular clothing and customs, nuns became easy targets for discrimination. Puritan and Protestant Americans found the mysterious habits of nuns and the elaborate vestments of priests to be objects of curiosity, and in some areas of the United States, they caused much controversy. Furthermore, women in general were placed under much scrutiny in early America. For instance, an early New Jersey law levied the same penalties as for practicing witchcraft against those who used perfumes, cosmetics, high-heeled shoes, or dentures in order to entice a man into marriage. In New England thirty-eight women were summoned to court for wearing silk, long hair, and other "excesses." Thus, female Catholic religious were particularly disdained both for their gender and for their Roman ties.

Anti-Catholic sentiments were found in other parts of the world as well. Otto von Bismarck (1815–1898), chancellor of the German Empire, requested that some Catholic religious communities abandon habits in exchange for being allowed to continue their work in schools. The superior of the Sisters of Christian Charity refused, replying: "Nothing in this world will make my sisters faithless to their vows, and so I could not accept your offer at such a price."[5] Following European examples like Balzac's *Droll Tales from the Abbeys of Touraine* and Diderot's *La Religieuse,* the American book *The Awful Disclosures of Maria Monk* fueled American suspicions of nuns. This sensationalistic work was released in 1836, immediately selling 250,000 copies. Although discredited as a hoax, its anonymous author presented "firsthand" information from behind convent walls, where secret tunnels allowed priests and monks to impregnate nuns, the latter smothering the babies resulting from these liaisons. These shocking propaganda tales caused outraged citizens to burn to the ground an Ursuline school at Charlestown, Massachusetts, in 1834. Luckily, others fared better. Ursulines in San Antonio, Texas, suffered so much harassment from townspeople that they decided to hold an open house, offering their convent for inspection. They allowed people to examine every area of their home and possessions and calmly answered insulting questions, eventually putting the people at ease about their lifestyle.[6]

Yet most women religious routinely avoided wearing their habits while traveling to avoid harassment. Some were so poor that they used flour sacks for a secular costume, attracting even more ridicule than if they had remained in habit. When a group of St. Joseph sisters visited an Ursuline convent in New Orleans, the residents warned them to change their clothes into secular dress before leaving the convent, or "people would think that some nuns had escape[d] from the convent."[7] Those orders that maintained the class distinction between lay and choir sisters were especially reviled. The antidemocratic notion of requiring one woman to wear a bonnet while others wore veils was too much for American sensibilities.

Even Church authorities discouraged sisters from wearing their habits in public at this time for safety reasons, yet some communities did so nonetheless. Braving hostility, they became courageous public witnesses to Catholics around them. The "holy habit" became a rallying point for some Catholics, a source of pride and comfort. Girls admired and respected those nuns who remained in religious dress, flocking to their convent doors in droves. It seemed that the more women religious battled violence and oppression with dignity and courage, the more they attracted new recruits.

Civil War Nurses

The American Civil War (1861–1865) offered Catholic Americans an opportunity to challenge negative attitudes toward them. Catholic men enlisted for combat, and women religious offered their services on the battlefield. At first, the anti-Catholic sentiments, which had plagued them for decades, remained in place during wartime. Respected nursing leader Dorothea Dix (1802–1887) did not support Catholic nurses. Ironically, her dress requirements for nurses were remarkably similar to the habit of the Catholic nun:

> No young ladies should be sent at all, but some who ... are sober, earnest, self-sacrificing, and self-sustained; who can bear the presence of suffering, and exercise entire self-control of speech and manner; who can be calm, gentle, quiet, active, and steadfast in duty.
>
> Their clothing should reflect their mature sensibility: "All nurses are required to be plain looking women. Their dresses must be brown or black, with no bows, no curls, no jewelry, and no hoopskirts."[8]

Some soldiers had never seen a nun's habit and responded to the startling clothing with hostility, hiding under blankets and refusing to allow sisters to touch them. Others spat and swore at them or even attacked them physically.

Nonetheless, the selfless actions of nuns toward both Confederate and Union troops soon tempered these hostile attitudes across the board. Doctors were impressed with the sisters' skill, discipline, respect for authority, and endurance. The habit served as a protection that enabled them to go places not suitable for unescorted women. Their willingness to risk great danger for their fellow Americans soon made them heroines. Although several Catholic priests who acted as chaplains for Confederate soldiers were killed during the war, no Catholic sisters or female nurses were killed or wounded by gunfire for the duration of the conflict. They were treated with great respect and always moved freely across enemy lines unharmed. There is evidence suggesting that Confederate spies used this ability to their advantage and disguised themselves in nuns' habits to engage in covert operations.[9] Mother Angela Gillespie (1824–1887) is regarded as having built and administered the best military hospital in the United States located in Mound City, Illinois, during the Civil War. President Abraham Lincoln wrote the following regarding the sisters:

> Of all forms of charity and benevolence seen in the crowded wards in the hospitals, those of some Catholic Sisters were among the most efficient. I never knew hence they came or what was the name of their Order.
>
> More lovely than anything I had ever seen in art, so long devoted to illustrations of love, mercy and charity, are the pictures that remain of those modest Sisters, going on their errands of mercy among the suffering and the dying. Gentle and womanly, yet with the courage of soldiers leading a forlorn hope, to sustain them in contact with such horror. As they went from cot to cot distributing the medicines proscribed, administering the cooling, refreshing, strengthening draughts as directed, they were veritable Angels of Mercy.
>
> Their words are suited to sufferer. One they incited or encouraged another they calmed and soothed. With every soldier conversed about his home, his wife, his children, all the loved ones he was soon to see again if he was obedient and patient.
>
> How many times have I seen them exorcise pain by their presence, by their words! How often has the hot forehead of the soldier grown cool as one of those Sisters bathed it! How often has he been refreshed, encouraged and assisted along the road of convalescence when he would otherwise have fallen by the way, by some home memories with which these unpaid nurses filled the heart. . . .[10]

After the war, Catholic nuns were able to wear their habits in public without fear of harassment, now receiving respect and courtesy from citizens everywhere. In 1924 a memorial was erected by the Ladies' Ancient Order of Hibernians to commemorate the nuns who served as nurses in the Civil War, located near the Lincoln Memorial in Washington, D.C. The habit of each order is represented in the granite sculpture, including the Sisters of St. Joseph, Sisters of St. Dominic, Ursuline Sisters, Holy Cross Sisters, Sisters of the Poor of St. Francis, Sisters of Charity of St. Vincent de Paul, Sisters of Charity of Mother Seton, Sisters of Charity of Nazareth, and Sisters of Providence of St. Mary of the Woods.

Beyond serving as battlefield nurses, women religious orders have surmounted endless obstacles to provide healthcare to staggering numbers of our nation's most needy citizens, founding institutions early in our history that continue to affect our lives today. St. Vincent's Hospital in New York is a prime example. Crucial in ministering to victims of the terrorist attacks of September 11, 2001, it was founded by four Sisters of Charity in 1849.

Nursing Habits

Although early medical sisters wore the same religious dress for all activities, the nursing occupation created changes in the habit based on requirements of the work. The Sisters of Bon Secours were founded in 1824 in France to provide home nursing. They were well known in Paris and in great demand, making home visits at a time when hospitals were so appalling that few individuals wished to be treated in them. Their habit included *les manchettes blanches* (small white linen cuffs), a detail suggested by the Archbishop de Quélen when the sisters cared for him during his own illness. The Bon Secours also wore a black wool shawl, tailored without fringe for novices. When cashmere became too expensive to use for the shawl, they obtained permission from Rome to utilize another medium-weight cloth. The fabric for their original blue aprons also became difficult to obtain, so the community switched to black. In America, the Sisters of Bon Secours were easily recognized by their distinctive white bonnets and black medical bags, which they carried on their rounds. Their patients mentioned that just the mere sight of these articles brought them immense comfort.[11]

American Holy Cross sisters wore a white cap, black habit, and long apron. Those working in hospitals wore white habits with narrower sleeves and fewer gathers in the skirt. Their bodices were more fitted, and they wore a short veil. Standard white nursing uniforms eventually would replace their white habits to make it easier and more hygienic for work. Secular nurses adopted a veil or modified nun's cap, and the title "Sister" became adopted in the British Empire for all nurses. Catherine McAuley (1778–1841) founded the Sisters of Mercy in Dublin, Ireland, to aid the underserved. She adopted an unobtrusive, uniform dress that was not intended as a habit. Yet their appearance and lifestyle made the Sisters of Mercy quite distinguishable, and they later formally established themselves as religious. In 1900 the socialite Rose Lathrop Hawthorne, the daughter of Nathaniel Hawthorne, established the St. Rose's Free Home for Incurable Cancer in New York City. She and her companions cut their hair and adopted a quasi-religious dress with a white neckerchief and cap similar to that worn by the Sisters of Charity. Later they adopted the traditional white Dominican habit, although as a convert to Catholicism, Hawthorne found the clothing to be strange. To this day, the Hawthorne Dominican sisters do not charge their patients, nor do they accept Medicare or Medicaid funds, relying completely on gifts of charity for their funding.[12]

In 1884 Mother Marianne Cope and the Sisters of St. Francis of Syracuse took charge of a leper hospital in Honolulu, Hawaii. When they arrived at the request of the famous Father Damian de Veuster, they found horrendous conditions. Patients of all ages and both sexes slept together on bloodstained mattresses on the floor; wards crawled with bedbugs, lice, and maggots. The stench of rotting flesh permeated the premises. Mother Marianne immediately improved the sanitary and social conditions of the patients, teaching her sisters how to nurse the foul sores of the unfortunate victims of the disease. She segregated family members who were not afflicted.

After Father Damian died from leprosy himself, Mother Marianne took over for him at the island of Molokai. She took charge of the bleak Bishop Home for Unprotected Leper Girls and Women, establishing a new standard of living for the inmates. Although Mother Marianne wore the plain, rough habit of a Franciscan nun, as a teenager in New York she had worked in a clothing factory and had a great sense of style. Rather than provide simple, drab uniforms for her patients, she fashioned beautiful clothing for them. One of the sisters recalled the following:

> The girls were dressed like New Yorkers. . . . Whatever she touched, tying a bow, trim a hat or make a dress to everything she gave an artistic touch. She was expert in the blending of colors. I would show her something I made and she would say the colors did not look well together. She took great pride in making dresses for the girls. It was Mother Marianne who bought the girls hair ribbons and pretty things to wear, dresses and scarves. Women keep their cottages and rooms in the big communal houses neatly, pridefully. There are snowy bedspreads, pictures on the walls. They set their tables at mealtimes with taste. She interested the leper women in harmony and color. Sit in service at the back of the church at Molokai and observe the lovely arrangement of color on the women. When Mother went to the island people there had no thought for the graces of life. We are lepers they told her what does it matter? She changed all that. Doctors have said that her psychology was 50 years ahead of its time.[13]

The novelist Robert Louis Stevenson happened to visit the island and observed Mother Marianne's extraordinary work. He was so impressed that a week after his stay, he had an elegant piano shipped to the community, wishing the sisters and the patients to have the benefit of music added to their pleasant surroundings.

Another example of courageous caregiving occurred thirty years earlier. Henriette Delille, a free woman of African descent, founded the Sisters of the Holy Family in New Orleans. The congregation of African American women dedicated their lives to caring for sick, elderly, and poor former slaves. They own and operate the oldest continuously operating Catholic home for the aged in the United States. Their community received pontifical status in 1842, decades before the Emancipation Proclamation, when slavery was still at its height in the South. Yet the idea of a black women appearing in the "holy habit" was so distasteful to some Catholics that the diocese of New Orleans forbade the sisters to wear their habits in public.[14]

The Oblates of Providence, the first African American congregation of Catholic nuns, faced similar prejudices. Founded by Sister Mary Elizabeth Lange (1784–1882) in 1829, the sisters walked the streets of Baltimore and Philadelphia in their religious habits only to be physically attacked and ridiculed. But Elizabeth triumphed over these trials, establishing a network of schools and orphanages. The Oblate Sisters of Providence continue to operate the oldest educational facility for black children in the United States.[15]

But white Catholics would feel a similar burden of discrimination as their black sisters. Children encountered the habit mainly in schools, where sisters made a tremendous impact on young Catholics in the nineteenth and twentieth centuries. Many bishops encouraged a parish to use funds to establish schools even before churches. Civic governments sometimes formed partnerships with Catholic schools to educate non-Catholic children. Townspeople were happy to receive the services of sisters, but many were unhappy about their religious garb.

In 1887 the State Board of New York ruled that sisters could not wear religious habits in public schools.[16] Those who did not follow this directive were let go that same year. These "antigarb" laws limited American Catholic sisters' ability to teach in public schools well into the twentieth century. The North Dakota legislature passed a law in 1948 forbidding public school teachers from wearing religious clothing or emblems, forcing the bishop to give nuns in the state special permission to wear secular clothing so that they might continue their work.

Nonetheless, Catholic sisters continued to open schools for children of diverse backgrounds, offering education as a means of self-improvement to persons who would otherwise not have the opportunity. Many orders ventured into new territories to establish schools against all odds. In 1870 Native American Chief Selstice of the Coeur d'Alenes wrote to the Sisters of Providence to request their services, clearly with no problem regarding their clothing:

> Dear Sister Catherine,
>
> Our hearts were full of joy when you passed through our country. Now I want you to come and live with us and teach our girls. Our Fathers, the Blackrobes, take care of our boys and we are glad; but our girls are orphans. They are ignorant and they will always be that way, unless you come and take care of them. When I went to see you, you made me so welcome that I could see how well you like the Indians; now I want to ask the chief of the women Blackrobes to give us Sisters. We will build a house for them and will help them. I beg the Great Spirit to fill your hearts with mercy for the poor Coeur d'Alene girls. Our Fathers, the Blackrobes teach us that the Big Chief on High gives plenty for a little charity to others. So the reward for the women Blackrobes will be very great if they come to open the eyes and hearts and the minds of our poor girls!

Yes, I hope the Great Spirit will touch your heart and open your ears to our prayers. Pray for me and for all my children.

Selstice, Chief of the Coeur d'Alenes.[17]

A school was opened in 1878.

Victorian Ideals

Religious life offered the opportunity for middle-class women to have meaningful careers when few other options existed. Non-Catholic women envied those who could join religious communities, where women were put into positions of responsibility and where they could acquire high levels of administrative and business skill without the scorn of their peers.

In secular society, however, well-bred Victorian women reared children and entertained themselves with genteel activities. Clothing in this era was designed deliberately to disguise the natural body, with high necks, padding, corsets, and voluminous fabric. An 1895 law in Chicago prohibited women from revealing their stockings when bicycling. In 1900 two ladies were arrested in Buffalo, New York, for raising their full-length skirts to cross a muddy street. Victorians replaced the word "leg" with "limb" and set about hiring artists to conceal exposed genitalia on their European artworks.

In 1877 the corset was worn so tight that normal movement was difficult. Men did not impose these articles of clothing, as some imagine—oddly, they were kept in vogue by women, even against pleas from the medical community of the day.[18] The Rational Dress movement, of which writer Oscar Wilde was a member, rallied against the corsets, padded bustles, and unnecessary layers, hoping to move the fashions of women to a more comfortable direction.

In some cases, the religious habit followed Victorian trends and as a result became more elaborate and cumbersome in design. The simple cap and dress of seventeenth- and eighteenth-century women religious gave way to more "dignified" designs. The idea of the upper classes redeeming the poor greatly appealed to Victorians, providing that social strata remained strictly delineated. Differences in the choir and lay habits maintained class distinctions that enabled some women to join communities who would not do so otherwise—it was socially acceptable for them to go into religious service as long as there remained a servant class in the organization.[19] Because some of these complicated, overly elaborate habits became part of the constitutions of orders, they lasted for decades. The black silk bonnet and cape of St. Elizabeth Anne Seton (1774–1821), founder of the American Sisters of Charity, could be seen on the streets as late as the 1960s.

Nuns' habits became an object of particular fascination in the pornography of the Victorian Age. Brothels kept nuns' habits on hand for customer requests, and the image of the whip-wielding nun was very popular at the time. In reality, some communities authorized use of the "discipline," a small whip with knotted cords used as a tool of self-inflicted penance. One was not permitted to use it with so much force that it drew blood. When not in use, it was kept in a small black bag in a sister's cell. One Carmelite community made its income from making these instruments, but they faded out of use in the twentieth century in all but the most austere communities.

Missionaries

Victorian attitudes toward the body and class distinctions were carried out into the mission field as well. Beginning as early as 1638, Catholic sisters traveled to the most remote corners of the earth to provide education, healthcare, and social services to those in need. Most Christian missionaries urged African, South American, and Asian peoples to cover their nudity and to adopt Western modes of dress. In some cases, natives complied, but, unaware of how to clean their new clothes, they suffered from infection as a result. In other cases, wearing wet garments caused illness in those who had not been trained about drying them.[20]

Western dress was sometimes completely unsuitable to mission climates and culture, and the habit was no exception. Although most orders that traditionally wore black garb switched to white in hot climates, the change did not always take place speedily since permission had to be obtained through a number of channels, beginning with the motherhouse and ultimately from either their local bishop or from Rome. When the Sacred Heart sisters founded operations in the Congo, they wore the same hot black woolen clothing they used in European winters. The Franciscan Sisters of Mary Immaculate order originated in Switzerland, and their heavy woolen garments remained standard dress in their missions in Equador and Colombia, including wearing in public a seven-part woolen cape that completely covered the habit.

Many sisters suffered from their inappropriate attire. Eventually concessions were made, so that mission versions of habits could be made from lighter materials and more streamlined designs. The Sisters of the Holy Cross adopted habits made from lightweight white materials when they traveled to Bangladesh; their long skirts were shortened, and in some cases their layered ensembles were exchanged for local native attire. They embraced a shorter veil when the heat and humidity made it impossible to maintain the starched folds of their elaborate fluted cap. In Nigeria, some orders changed to shorter dresses and bright, colored headscarves because the local people were so put off by the habit. The color black, which had negative connotations in Nigerian culture, particularly frightened children.[21] The Sisters of Providence created a modified habit for sisters in Argentina where high winds sometimes endangered sisters who traveled in their long, flowing garments. The new style resembled a nurse's uniform, with a shorter skirt and veil.

Contemplative nuns also traveled to foreign lands. The Poor Clares established convents in the Holy Land, and the Visitation nuns traveled to Syria. Both the Cistercians and Carmelites established cloistered convents in the Far East. Asian women easily identified with the withdrawn, introspective idea of cloistered life, and many Hindu and Buddhist nuns changed into Western habits and joined the European orders upon their conversion to Catholicism.

The Sisters of Loretto encouraged Chinese women to abandon their custom of foot binding, to modernize their hairstyles, and to appear in public. Local women were urged to form their own branches of religious communities, although this kind of growth was sometimes hindered by the insistence on their adopting the European dress of the motherhouse. Yet some orders did not insist on imposing dress and customs that were too far removed from native cultures and tried to adapt their norms to that of the culture they served. In 1867 the Presentandines founded the Helpers of Holy Souls, Chinese sisters who continued to wear their native dress while working among the poor in schools and healthcare facilities. In 1574, when Sister Marie de la Croix of the Sisters of St. Joseph de Cluny accepted three sisters from the tropics, she designed a habit for them based on local dress:

> It is fresh, original and magnificent, simple and right for the country. Imagine our three black daughters with their heads bare and their hair forming a black halo around their black faces, a long floating dress in the fashion of the country but held at the waist by a belt with long sleeves and buttoned to the wrist (it is strange that all dresses among the blacks have short sleeves). They wear a bib like ours but similar to the dress; our little white collar with blue cord and the medallion of the third order. This is the costume, all blue, the blue of the society.[22]

When the Sisters of St. Joseph of the Apparition established houses in Algeria, they abolished the distinction between lay and choir sisters when the Algerians strongly reacted against the notion of some sisters wearing gold rings while others wore silver ones. It seemed to them that this hierarchical difference meant that the lay sisters were being punished in some way. As a result, the whole system was subsequently abandoned.[23]

Mother Teresa of Calcutta (1910–1997) founded the Missionaries of Charity in 1950, creating a habit for the women religious made from the same inexpensive white cotton fabric used by the lower class in India. Rather than copying the design from the traditional habit of the Sisters of Loretto, her former order, she chose to fashion her habit as a sari pinned with a crucifix. The simple, modest covering of the sari and veil was edged with a blue border, in honor of the Blessed Virgin. In India, white is considered a color of mourning, so the habit of the Missionaries of Charity reflected their separation from the world. The habit includes a rope cincture, representing the Virgin Mary's purity; sandals; and a Rosary. The habit reflected Mother Teresa's love for the lowest and poorest of society, and it continues to be worn all over the world to this day.[24]

Twentieth-Century Struggles

In 1901 the Church formally recognized all women's religious communities as "true" religious. (Up to that point, those institutes that practiced apostolic works and did not remain in the cloister were considered as a separate class of sister.) As a result, nuns from all traditions came under the jurisdiction of the Code of Canon Law issued in 1917, which dictated many aspects of their lifestyle and dress. All habits were now required to meet with the approval of Rome or the local bishop. The 1917 code featured numerous specific regulations about the religious habit. It required religious to wear the habit at all times unless a competent superior judged otherwise. It forbade new communities to adopt the habit of an approved institution. Other rules stipulated that novices wear the habit of the institute but forbade postulants to do so.

To maintain distinctions between communities, many habits had taken on bizarre characteristics, requiring excessive attention to minutiae. Many new congregations elected to create simple, tailored habits quite unlike their predecessors. The American Missionary Servants of the Most Blessed Trinity, founded in 1912, in Baltimore, Maryland, did not wear a veil, for example. World War I caused the previously elaborate Edwardian fashions of secular society to become more streamlined and tailored, especially among those women who were involved with wartime activities, as extravagances would have seemed out of place. Some religious orders followed this trend, adopting a "uniform" approach to the habit. In Chicago in 1918 the Missionary Catechists of Our Lady of Victory wore a simple navy blue dress with a white collar and cuffs, a simple veil, and a silver medal of our Lady of Victory on a silver chain around their necks. The Social Mission Sisters worked in the slums of Cleveland wearing a tailored black dress and black hat along with a gold ring engraved with the letters "I.H.S." (monogram of the name of Jesus Christ) as their only insignia. The Society of Christ the King wore a modern dress and hat along with a crucifix on a neck chain. The Ladies of Bethany, founded in the Netherlands in 1919, wore secular clothing with no religious emblems whatsoever and used the title "Miss" rather than "Sister."[25]

After the war, methods in clothing manufacturing advanced. Travel became easier, and homes began to have modern plumbing and heating. Heavy layers were no longer required for warmth. The short skirt, which came into vogue in Western secular society around 1925, scandalized religious and political leaders alike. The Archbishop of Naples blamed a recent earthquake at Amalfi on God's anger over a skirt that did not cover the knee. Utah legislators tried unsuccessfully to pass a bill to regulate the length of skirts for all females over the age of fourteen. At first the androgynous look became fashionable, with dropped waists, flattened chests, and boyish haircuts. This fad did not last; by the 1930s evening clothing exposed much of the naked back or emphasized the shape of the buttocks.

The period after World War I was an era of great expansion for the Catholic Church worldwide. Large numbers of new parishes and schools sprang up. New religious orders emerged from the sheer numbers of women educated in the parochial system where they were exposed to religious life, whose purpose at this time was serving the people of God through education, hospital care, and social services. At the beginning of World War II, there were an unprecedented number of religious women throughout the globe.

Nazi Terror

St. Edith Stein (1891–1942) recognized the threat of Nazism even before it was a threat to others in her German homeland. She began her career as an exceptionally brilliant Jewish scholar, writer, and teacher, earning her doctorate in philosophy summa cum laude at a time when women rarely advanced in this field. In 1922 her study of the life of St. Teresa of Ávila inspired her to convert to Catholicism. By 1933 she joined the Carmelites and took the name Sister Teresa Benedicta of the Cross. As a nun, she astutely petitioned Catholic officials in several countries to rally against the imminent threat to the Jews in their lands. She has since been canonized by the Roman Catholic Church.

Many women religious who remain unrecognized also assisted their Jewish compatriots to escape the Nazi threat. Because of their cloistered way of life, convents became refuges for Jewish citizens. As late as 1943, the chief rabbi of Florence, Italy, urged Jews to flee to small villages or convents under false Christian names. Catholic monasteries, schools, and orphanages throughout Europe sheltered people, particularly children, and systematically provided Jews with false identities, food ration cards, and funds for travel.

In Poland the Sisters of Maria, Ursulines, and Franciscan sisters, among others, offered asylum to Jewish children. Approximately 190 convents participated in these relief efforts. Irene Sendler, a social worker in Warsaw who rescued thousands of Jewish children, attributes her success rate to the sisters. She remembered that no sister ever refused to take in a child. At the Jewish ghetto of Pruzhany in Bellorussia, nuns saved Jewish women from the death camps by disguising them in the habits of the order.

And women religious went even further. Mother Donata of the Instituto Palazzo in Milan helped hundreds cross the border to Switzerland. Benedictine Sister Margit Slachta traveled to Rome to ensure the safety of Jewish Hungarians, resulting in a church directive that all Benedictine convents and other church institutions in Hungary throw open their doors to help refugees. Anna Borkowska, superior of a Polish Benedictine convent, organized her sisters as secret agents and provided weapons to the underground. They easily traveled to homes and farms under the pretense of Church business, procured armaments, and hid them in their long habits, returning to their convent without raising suspicion. Holocaust historian Philip Friedman said of these sisters: "The hands accustomed to the touch of rosary beads became expert with explosives."[26]

New Regimes

While the habit continued to enjoy respect in the United States and Western Europe, it did not fare as well in other lands. Religious persecution raged in Mexico in the late 1920s. The state had seized administrative authority over priests—churches became state property, and parochial education was outlawed. Any manner of religious dress was illegal, and wearing the religious habit could warrant the death penalty. The law prohibiting religious habits existed in Mexico for several decades. Religious orders disbanded, with members going into hiding or fleeing the country.

Mother Maria Luisa Josepha, a Mexican Carmelite superior, arranged to take two sisters to America to escape this persecution. As they boarded the train in Guadalajara, they were dressed like any of the other passengers, including high heels, to make sure no one would recognize them as Carmelite sisters. At one point, a tunnel collapsed, forcing the passengers to walk a mile to another train. Mother Maria Luisa Josepha remarked to her sisters the folly of her high heels, longing for her Carmelite sandals. When the three finally arrived in Los Angeles, they immediately returned to their coarse brown habits and black veils, now symbols of religious freedom that caused great rejoicing among them.[27]

Sisters joining the Daughters of St. Francis of Assisi in Central Europe did so in secret. Unable to wear the habit, they wore lay clothing instead while working at and living in small groups in separate apartments. Their American sisters recognized this to be a great sacrifice, as the women greatly desired to live in community and wear the habit. After the fall of the communist government, the entire congregation had a meeting in Slovakia, the place of their origin, and reunited the congregation by adapting a distinct habit. In 1995 the sisters adopted the habit they wear today—a handsome black pleated dress with a simple white collar and soft, short black veil, and a Franciscan medal that depicts the Franciscan Tau cross, the bare arm of Christ, and the sleeved arm of St. Francis.[28]

In communist countries where the habit was allowed, it served as a shield for the wearers. One Maryknoll sister related:

> ... in the course of our various works, how many Sisters have found themselves in places and situations where it was unsafe for a young woman to be. Yet, even licentious and lewd men with no respect for women, have a superstitious fear of touch-

ing a consecrated woman. Our Sisters who have been in such situations and in communist prisons can testify to the saving power of the religious habit. They would not have had that protection in secular clothes.

The need for courage would manifest itself further in subsequent decades.

CHAPTER EIGHT

Explosion

*B*y the 1950s and 1960s, there was huge demand all over the world for the teaching and nursing services provided by women religious. American women's religious orders administered 850 hospitals, over 100 colleges, thousands of schools, and a vast network of social institutions and missionary outposts. Women entered religious life in record numbers, and there were more Catholic sisters than at any other time in history, even before the French Revolution.

Catholic sisters had become a highly visible and recognizable group of caregivers who responded to the needs of the marginalized in every strata of contemporary society, and the nun's habit had become recognized and respected by more people than ever before. Yet the attire reflected another time. Many religious saw the habit as antiquated clothing that now symbolized remoteness from the very society they strove to serve. Habits that had originated as copies of peasant garb or replicas of the costumes of a foundress had become for some a barrier to ministering to the world.

It was not only women religious who were concerned about the unsuitability of their clothing in the modern world. On September 13, 1951, Pope Pius XII addressed a group of sisters, saying: "With regard to the religious habit, choose one that expresses your interior lack of affectation, simplicity, and religious modesty." A year later he noted at the First International Congress of Superiors General of Orders and Congregations of Women:

> The religious habit should always express the consecration of Christ; that is expected and desired by all. By other respects the habit should be appropriate and in keeping with the demands of hygiene. We could not refrain from expressing our satisfaction at the fact that during the course of a year a few congregations had already taken some practical steps in this matter. To sum up: in things that are not essential make the adaptations counseled by reason and well-ordered charity.

Shortly after the pope's unprecedented pronouncement, *Life* magazine featured reprints of drawings from top Italian fashion designers who offered new habit design ideas for the Italian magazine *Il Tempo*. These creations ranged from practical and modern ensembles to haute couture. Designer Mamelie Barbara presented an ensemble that included a halo-shaped hat, a slim, gray flannel gown with dolman sleeves, and a sash that closely resembled a priest's stole. Another featured a swing-style dress and kerchief tied around the head. Other designs resembled clerical costumes, nurses' uniforms, or various contemporary secular fashions.[1]

Most women's religious orders rejected these ideas entirely, and some found the Vatican's interest in their clothing to be nothing short of meddlesome. Nevertheless, nuns around the world began at least to consider changes to the habit. Hoping to lead the way, the pope simplified the cardinals' official costume, cutting in half the twenty-foot-long copes so that they would no longer require trainbearers. He also made allowances for part of the cardinal's costume to be fabricated from wool rather than the original watered silk, cutting the minimum cost of each ensemble from $3,000 to $2,000.[2]

The first women's religious community to respond to the pope's call for simplicity was the Religious of Nazareth, who chose to simplify their collars and veils. Other groups followed with similar small changes. Most sisters, however, were reluctant to institute even the slightest changes to their holy habits. Since many nuns felt that it was scandalous to remove the habit even for swimming or convent plays and pageants, the idea of altering its design was truly abhorrent. Thus, most established orders kept their habits intact. It was not until 1959 that the Sacred Congregation for Religious demanded for reasons of safety that a sister whose work necessitated the driving of an automobile modify her headgear to allow for clear vision of the road.[3]

On the other hand, new religious orders that formed after the pope's appeal tended to choose more up-to-date habits. The American Sisters of the Divine Spirit, for example, were founded in 1954 and chose a gray skirt, white blouse with Peter Pan collar, nylon stockings, black leather pumps, and a flat felt hat. Their ensemble included a religious medal unique to the community. While some newly formed institutes adhered to older forms of the habit, they often chose shortened and streamlined versions of the tunic and veil; for example, the Marian Society of Dominican Catechists, founded in 1954 in Louisiana, adopted a basic Dominican habit shortened twelve inches from the floor and replaced the traditional veil with a simple black lace mantilla.[4]

The 1950s were the beginning of a radical transformation in the lives of many women religious the world over. This was the case particularly in the United States, where sisters not only scrutinized their clothing options but began to evaluate all other areas of their lives as well. Some questioned the rationale behind barring women religious from watching television or from reading the newspaper, for example, when they actually were deeply involved with secular society through their work. Moreover, religious duties of fixed hours of prayer and other convent activities began to seem at odds with modern work responsibilities and schedules.

In 1950 Pope Pius XII stated in his papal bull, *Sponsa Christi*, that modern religious could no longer depend on the income from land gifts and that they must devise ways of making their living by other appropriate enterprises. Although sisters were supposed to maintain a primary occupation of prayer and honoring God, the pope made it clear that sisters must begin to embrace the professional world. The Sister Formation Conference took place in 1954 to encourage religious communities to train nuns in various fields according to contemporary professional standards. The conference was an important catalyst in propelling sisters into the modern age. Through its publication, the *Sister Formation Bulletin,* it linked thousands of women religious together and informed them about new ideas and attitudes toward religious life. Furthermore, *Sponsa Christi* encouraged sisters to adapt all areas of religious life to modern needs and for communities to form federations. In 1956 the Vatican's Congregation for Religious asked U.S. sisters to form a national conference, which resulted in the formal establishment of the Conference of Major Superiors of Women (CMSW). The organization's goals were to advance the spiritual welfare of American women religious; increase the effectiveness of their work; and promote closer cooperation with all religious in the United States, the clergy, the Catholic hierarchy, and other religious associations.

Vatican II

In January 1959 Pope John XXIII announced that he had been inspired by the Holy Spirit to call the Second Vatican Council with the objective of making the Church and message of Jesus Christ more easily understandable and more relevant to the modern world. The Council opened on October 11, 1962, under his leadership. He stated, "We are going to shake off the dust that has collected on the throne of Saint Peter since the time of Constantine and let in some fresh air." This idea was often described with the Italian term *aggiornamento,* meaning "updating." Another guiding concept of the Council was the idea of *resourcement* (French for "return to the sources"), as the Council sought to recover the earliest roots of the faith from the teachings of Scripture and the Fathers of the Church. Overall, Vatican II stressed the importance of internal rather than external changes. In terms of religious life, for example, Vatican II particularly emphasized the connection between consecrated persons and the needs of the poor. Hundreds of religious orders began to consider how they might reshape their communities to make themselves more useful to the world.

No members of women's religious orders were permitted to participate in the Council, and none attended the first two sessions. After the death of Pope John XXIII in 1963, his successor, Pope Paul VI, said, "We believe that the time has come for the religious life of women to be given more honor and to be made more efficacious." As a result, a limited number of sisters were invited to audit the 1964 and 1965 sessions. Yet they were not allowed to participate even in matters that directly and exclusively affected their lives. Some sisters believed that their presence at the Council was greatly inhibited by the image that their habits projected. Of women present at the sessions, theology professor Carmel McEnroy, RSM, commented in her book *Guests in Their Own House: The Women of Vatican II*:

> A challenge was to get past the idea of the "good sister" who looked like an adult doll in the dress of another age. It was difficult to discover the real person of the individual sister and take her seriously when she was seen in the mass-produced habit that suggested she was a carbon copy of all her other dressalikes, leaving her little personal identity beyond "one of the sisters."[5]

Habits Must Change

In the same year as the opening of Vatican II, Léon Joseph Cardinal Suenens, Archbishop of Malines-Brussels, Belgium, published his

The Nun in the World, a revolutionary book that examined women's religious life in modern times. He spoke about the habit in this way:

> The world today has no patience with mere ornamentation, offerings and other oddities, whether starched or floating in the wind, which belong to another age: anything contrived or lacking in simplicity is rejected, and anything unpractical or unhygienic, anything that gives the impression that the nun is not only apart from the world but also a complete stranger to its evolution.

The Second Vatican Council reached similar conclusions. In October 1965 the Decree on the Appropriate Renewal of the Religious Life, *Perfectae caritatis,* stated:

> The religious habit, as a symbol of consecration, must be simple and modest, at once poor and becoming. In addition, it must be in keeping with the requirements of health and it must be suited to the times and place and to the needs of the apostolate. The habits, both of men and women, which are not in conformity with these norms ought to be changed.

By this time, some orders, such as the School Sisters of Notre Dame and the Sisters of the Third Order of St. Francis, had already completely overhauled their habits. The missionary Canonesses of St. Augustine changed their clothing as well as their name when they became the Missionary Sisters of the Immaculate Heart of Mary in 1964. They replaced their original white serge habit and spectacular headdress with a simple and attractive dress, belted scapular, and plain black veil with a narrow white edging pushed back on the head, allowing some of their hair to show. That same year the Ursulines, who at their origin in the sixteenth century had worn contemporary dress, changed from a traditional habit to a modern work uniform consisting of a dark skirt and a vest embroidered with their motto "Only for the Glory of God."[6] In January 1965 all Sacred Heart nuns were asked to relinquish their gold profession rings, which would be sold for a contribution to the Holy Father's charity.[7]

Habit changes among orders varied widely. Some habits altered gradually over time while others transformed quickly. In a 1965 Catholic magazine article, Holy Cross Sister Charles Borromeo noted that diverse attitudes toward updating the habit ranged from those who "pray for death before habit changes" to those who were eager and enthusiastic to don secular attire and embrace the world. Generally, it was the younger sisters, particularly in America, who were eager for swift metamorphosis, while older religious and those in European countries continued to resist proposed updates.

In October 1966 the pope issued a *motu proprio* (a decree, literally "of his own accord") to the superiors of religious orders, which specified procedures for instituting the decrees of the Second Vatican Council. He mandated that within three years, all major superiors must convene a special chapter, or committee, to recommend a path of renewal for their communities. His letter encouraged experimentation and made allowances for orders' Vatican-approved constitutions to be replaced by temporary bylaws drawn up by sisters.

Some sisters visited dress and shoe shops to gather updating ideas, while others turned to professionals for advice. The Daughters of Charity turned to top fashion designer Christian Dior for their first modifications; he presented them with a box-pleated dress and kerchieflike veil attached to a stiff, squared-off white frame. The American Sisters of Charity approached Marguery Burke Bolhagen of Bergdorf Goodman, who designed a new habit for them, which was at first made at the store and later by Fitzpatrick's, a New York manufacturer of nuns' apparel. The Sisters of Mercy commissioned designer Sibyl Connolly, who created for them a simple, long-sleeved navy dress with a white collar and short black veil.[8]

Sometimes this process was reversed, and designers approached sisters with unsolicited ideas. In his New York boutique, Paraphernalia, Walter Holmes featured nun and monk minidresses that he named "mini-medievals." Holmes expected rave reviews from sisters and offered his creations in gray, royal blue, and white. No orders adopted his minihabits, but a new community of Benedictine monks in Wisconsin hired him to design a streamlined contemporary version of their traditional habit. Some communities of sisters who worked with the urban poor, however, seriously debated whether to adopt miniskirts to identify better with those whom they served.[9] The Maryknoll sisters solicited professional advice from a panel of home economics experts for their proposed new design. One comment on an early modified habit said, "As I read over the requirements for religious garb outlined by Vatican II that you have given me, I think your present habit is not fulfilling of it in the area of practicality for your work, especially in Hawaii. The Sisters are constantly putting back their capes to write on the blackboard and to work. You look hot and cumbersome." The Maryknolls systematically tested approved designs on all body shapes, taking care that even the "largest"-bosomed sister in the community would look attractive rather than dowdy in the proposed ensemble.[10]

Communities took the matter of updating the habit very seriously, spending hundreds of hours on fashion shows, correspondence, meetings, polling, and balloting. Given that most orders at this time were part of international federations, their internal communications about clothing had to span continents before changes might become implemented, and often directives about the habit were quite complicated. A group of Idaho Benedictines received 168 recommendations from their specially appointed Clothing Committee. Regarding experimentation, for example, the committee offered the following guidelines:

1. One must be able to use present habit material to do the experiment.
2. One must be able to do the sewing herself.
3. The design or pattern one chooses must be presented to the

Clothing Committee for approval. Include with the pattern a list of incidentals needed—zippers, fasteners, facing, stiffening, buttons, etc. Permission for new fabrics must be obtained from Mother. The patterns approved by the committee will be forwarded to Mother for permission to make the experiment. When the committee approves the pattern or design, this also gives the local Superior permission to purchase the incidentals requested.

4. The only colors considered are black and white. The stockings must remain black. The length of the skirt must be a few inches below the knees, the skirt full so that the knees are covered when you sit down.

5. There may be no soliciting of material, money or accessories from relatives or friends. All of these will be provided by the community for the sisters.

6. Each sister who does an experiment is asked to do the following: a) Keep an account of costs, time spent in sewing, time spent in upkeep—laundering, pressing, etc. b) To report back to the committee next summer on the advantages and disadvantages of her particular style. Let us not lose sight of the purpose and experiment. It is to help us make a better choice when the time comes so that no money, time or material will be wasted. The Clothing Committee has been appointed to handle all suggestions and requests regarding clothing styles.[11]

Female religious superiors also sought help from charm schools and dress consultants to acclimate their sisters to modern expectations of appearance and behavior. Convents approached experts from airline stewardess schools and cosmetic companies such as Estée Lauder for instruction. Sisters received counseling on choosing styles of clothing that would suit their current needs as well as training in carrying themselves according to modern standards—they needed to learn how to rest their arms naturally at their sides, for example, rather than having them tucked behind long scapulars.[12]

Nuns whose headdresses were removed or replaced experienced many trials. As mentioned earlier, their hair was often thin and patchy from years of lack of oxygen and rubbing against fabric. Many experienced the use of their peripheral vision for the first time since their youth. One sister recalled getting sinus and throat infections so often without her veil that her doctor recommended wearing a hat until her body could adjust its internal thermostat. A Sister of Providence recalled: "And the interim habit . . . it made many of us look like a sack of flour tied in the middle! Nevertheless it was great to have neck and face free to feel the breeze."

For some sisters, body weight became an issue for the first time. No longer could figures remain hidden behind voluminous tunics. Many nuns went on diets. Others were faced with new decisions about hair, jewelry, and makeup, wishing to blend into secular society while at the same time remaining true to their vows of poverty and chastity. If earrings and lipstick were part of the standard professional business suit look, for example, then it seemed necessary to wear them. Yet these details caused so much uproar among the clergy and laity that the smallest decisions about appearances became very complicated.

During experimental stages, some individual sisters were permitted to design their own habits. Many attempts to update religious garb led to unattractive results. Habits that were simply shortened and streamlined without professional design input often ended up looking dowdy and ill-conceived. Those religious women who chose secular clothes often shopped at thrift stores or restricted themselves to hand-me-downs, either out of necessity or as a deliberate witness to their poverty. This kind of clothing often made them appear outmoded and shabby, inspiring concern about the image they projected for their community and to potential recruits. In many cases, these pieced-together outfits seemed more old-fashioned than the habits they replaced.[13]

The World Reacts

Changes that came slowly at first soon swept through convents. In 1965 there were 180,000 women religious, 105,000 of whom were teaching 4.5 million Catholic children annually. Youngsters who had up until then been taught to be in awe of the habit—sometimes even dressing in miniature versions for school pageants—were obviously disconcerted by the changes. Letters had to be sent home to parents and schoolchildren explaining the changes in attire, such as this one from the archives of the Congregation of Sisters, Servants of the Immaculate Heart of Mary, written by Sister Mary Avelina on September 30, 1966:

> Tomorrow, your teachers, the Sisters of the Immaculate Heart of Mary, will come to school dressed in the modified habit of the Sisters of our Community.
>
> Now what do we mean by modified?—Changed, of course, but not a drastic change. You will still see the blue habit and scapular, characteristic of our Sisters. It will be modified in this manner—the habit will be a few inches shorter, the sleeves, narrower, and the white collar will be smaller. The headdress, too will be modified. There will be no band on the forehead and the bonnet will be more off the face. The change in the veil is not noticeable.
>
> Now, why am I telling you this today. First, I want you to be able to give intelligent answers to those who will surely question you. One of the questions might be—Why are religious orders either modifying or changing their habits. Each one of you is familiar with at least some of the recommendations of Vatican II. Perhaps, those pertaining to the liturgy are better known.

Now, what about the many religious orders in the Church. They, too, must re-evaluate present day religious life in the light of the recent Ec. Council, Vatican II. This involves change or modification of attire to meet present day work of religious. The change is particularly notable in communities of Sisters founded in the 18th and 19th centuries and before. Today young women who enter the convent do so—not to escape the world, but to be a greater part of it by service to others. Sisters today work in many fields that Sisters of the 18th and 19th century never dreamed of. Today the Sister is eager to devote herself to such commitments.

Since Sisters are now serving in many areas and working more closely with the laity, religious community representatives have seen the necessity of a more modified dress or habit.

The Sisters who teach you in your school are dedicated to the active life, rather than the contemplative. They have gradually made changes to fit in with the present day. (Necessity of driving cars, attendance at meetings and speaking at assemblies.) So please explain this to those who might question you. And feel free to question the Sisters if you don't understand. Don't believe every comment you read in the daily paper, but get your information from the right source. Before long your Sisters will be doing some of the above. This week one of our Sisters, Sister Phillip, will be on a panel with other sisters of the diocese. They will speak before the priests of this deanery.

Some notes—from our Catholic Directory there are 23,000 Roman Catholic priests in the U.S.; 22,000 seminarians; 12,000 brothers; 101,000 Sisters. 250,000 Americans live according to the vows.

So tomorrow, the Sisters will look different, but not really so different. They will be the same. They are dedicated to be of service to you in the modern world, according to the recommendations of Vatican II.[14]

The modification of sisters' habits was of huge interest to the general public. Major secular newspapers and magazines across the globe reported the updates—headlines such as "Catholic Sisters Switch 134-Year-Old Costume" and "Nuns Model Drip-Dry Habits and Nylons in a Fashion Show" appeared in the *New York Times*. Hundreds of articles appeared in Catholic periodicals and diocesan bulletins debating the issues surrounding the updating of the habit. The secretary general of the Sacred Congregation for Religious and Secular Institutes received stacks of mail from religious who cried out against some of these new ideas, which they considered in excess of the guidelines of renewal.[15]

Many lay Catholics, too, were outraged or upset about the updating of habits. Of all of the changes to religious life, the habit was the most dramatic because it was so visible. Religious clothing had always been an important and respected sacramental to the laity. People were taught to stand up when a nun entered the room, for example, out of respect for the habit. It was considered holy clothing and possessed for many Catholics a singular beauty and nobility unmatched by other Church symbols. Many in secular society looked on cutting or altering the habit as an affront to the dignity of religious life. Several studies done in the 1960s indicated that the laity were very much against the idea of secular attire for Catholic sisters. Children who watched their sister-teachers transform often were disconcerted. Columnist Dr. Marian Horvat recalls:

> I along with my best friend Judy wanted to be nuns. Judy, who had more of a fashion sense than I, collected pictures of various habits to see which one appealed to her most. But for me, there was never a doubt. I would be a Sister of Charity—with their box habits. They were what I knew and loved. In seventh grade—after Vatican II—the nuns appeared in modified habits. We had the New Mass, and I lost all interest in becoming a sister like the ones I was seeing then.

Often men reacted the strongest. Author Marcelle Bernstein quotes one male interviewee's statement: "It was as if I had encountered a maiden aunt in hot pants." In 1970 author Sara Harris featured the following from an interview with a nun in her book *The Sisters: The Changing World of the American Nun*:

> I had a frightening experience last month with a policeman I knew when I was teaching two years ago. I came back to a congress at the school I'd taught in and this cop was there, and he was physically shaken when he saw me in a skirt and blouse. He grabbed me and said, "I can't stand to see you out of the habit. You are just terrible, and if you were my sister, I would beat you up." I wish I could describe to you how upset and furious he was about the whole thing—just because we're doing our thing as we believe Christ would have us doing it.[16]

In 1970 two psychologists from Boston College published a study on attitudes toward sisters who had adopted lay dress. Their report found that those participants with conservative political ideals reacted negatively to lay dress and those who were more politically liberal welcomed the change in nuns' clothing.[17] These attitudes reflected the spirit of the times, when secular society was likewise split on issues surrounding the civil rights movement, feminism, and the Vietnam War. In other surveys, younger people generally reacted well to sisters in secular clothing, perceiving their clothing choices as working along with the desires of Vatican II. The elderly disapproved, however, perceiving these modern women religious to be in defiance of the Holy See. In Sara Harris's book about American nuns, another sister recalls this incident:

> Only recently I was coming home from New York on the train, doing my own meditation and this kind of elderly dried-up woman sat down beside me. I knew she didn't approve of me. She began talking about my habit right away. She asked me if

I liked it and I said yes, I did, very much. She asked me why and I told her about its being a symbol for renewal, part of throwing off the useless tradition that had hampered us in our relationships with people. I made a point of telling her we intended to hold on to all the wonderful positive traditions.

Well, I could see her growing more and more indignant with me and my habit. I signified a certain aspect of renewal in the Church she obviously wasn't impressed with. By now, she was nearly livid and she shook her finger at me and said, "Someday the Pope is going to say to you and your kind, *"As you were!"*[18]

Habits Disappear Altogether

In a 1970 article in *Catholic Digest* entitled "Who Cares How Nuns Dress?" a priest suggested slacks for sisters as a practical and modest alternative to the modified habit that would unite them with the poor women whom they served. For some Catholics, the overall meaning of the habit began to come into question. Many sisters believed that merely to update a costume that at its core cut off religious from the world and that symbolized a way of life and thinking that was becoming obsolete presented a problem. Moreover, they began to view the imposition of the habit as a form of oppression against women. Carmel McEnroy, RSM, wrote about this incident:

> Sister Alphonsus Brady asked me to model for the group a modified habit that we were thinking of adopting in the United States. It was a princess line black dress with a white collar and came well below my knees. I also wore a black veil with white trim, and I think my hair was showing slightly . . . as I approached, I could hear comments like "Here comes the mannequin." As I was then practically taken apart with eyes

and hands, someone told me, "That's no habit. It's a girl's dress." Then I faced his lordship the bishop and the six mother superiors. No one said anything. Finally Cahal B., as we fondly called him, blinked his eyes, nervously adjusted his glasses, and said, "Thank you sister. You may leave now." Then and there I decided that I would never again ask anyone about what I should wear.[19]

At this time, to maintain its canonical status, each religious order had to submit a revised constitution to the Congregation for Religious Institutes of Religious Life (CICL). The CICL acted as the administrative arm of the Vatican responsible for the oversight of religious institutes. Many sisters in the United States thought that because the CICL was composed of mostly non-American, all-male clergy, their needs would not be properly understood and addressed. One well-known confrontation over the habit between sisters and the Church hierarchy involved the California Institute of the Sisters of the Most Holy and Immaculate Heart of the Blessed Virgin Mary. They were considered a "progressive" order even in the 1940s, and early on, these sisters had been experimenting with nontraditional living arrangements, occupations, and clothing. As a result of their interpretations of Vatican II directives, they proposed to facilitate renewal in their community by allowing sisters to return to using their birth names and to wear more suitable work clothing. The archbishop of their diocese, Cardinal MacIntyre, believed that their proposals were inconsistent with the meaning of religious life, and he ordered the sisters' experimentation stopped. They refused. He then insisted that they comply or withdraw from service in the diocese. The sisters did not receive the backing of the Council of Major Superiors of Women, and their superior, Anita Caspary (Mother Mary Humiliata), was advised by other American bishops to "Pay lip service—have a habit, keep it in your closet, and wear it once a year on feast days."[20] Caspary believed that following this line of thought would be hypocritical, and the sisters' renewal constitution document stated:

> Women around the world, young and old, are playing decisive roles in public life, changing their world, developing new lifestyles. What is significant about this new power for women is not that it will always be for the good, nor that it will always edify, but that there can be no reversing of it now. Women who want to serve and who are capable of service have already given evidence that they can no longer uncritically accept the judgement of others as to where and how that service might be extended. American religious women want to be in the mainstream of this new, potentially fruitful, and inevitable bid for self-determination by women.[21]

The conflict ended in 1968, when a papal investigation mandated that the sisters obey their bishop. As a result, 260 of the 310 sisters left the order along with Caspery to form a noncanonical community.

Generally, those communities that made more gradual changes experienced less conflict within their organizations. Other communities made their clothing and lifestyle modifications according to Vatican directives with less-publicized but no less dramatic outcomes, with many communities split down the middle over issues involving the habit. Sisters either found themselves forced out of the habit against their wishes or in the position of forcing others to do so. Elderly and infirm nuns especially were unable to understand the new directives about clothing and in some cases believed they were being kicked out of their orders when asked to trade in their habits for new models or secular clothing. Habit modification caused great pain and suffering for those who saw the habit as the ultimate symbol of their lives. Even those who welcomed the changes found it to be an extremely emotionally draining process.

Rome Pulls Back the Reins

The first American community of sisters to abandon the traditional habit was the Sisters of Loretto, who adopted suits in the spring of 1966. Their mother general was Sister Luke Tobin, the only American nun to be invited to audit sessions of the Second Vatican Council. In 1967 the Congregation for Religious confirmed that American bishops and local ordinaries had the authority to determine whether religious superiors in their dioceses were using sufficiently grave motives for waiving the wearing of religious garb. However, in 1969 Rome's instructions on religious formation, *Renovationis causam*, perhaps added confusion to the matter in stating that novices no longer had to receive the habit. Yet the Vatican remained opposed to the practice of wholesale abandonment except for rare exceptions. Pope Paul VI issued an apostolic exhortation entitled *Evangelica testificatio* on June 29, 1971, that stated: "While we recognize that certain situations can justify not wearing a religious type of dress, we cannot fail to mention how fitting it is for the dress to be as the Council wishes, a sign of their consecration and in some way different from secular fashion." In 1972 the Sacred Congregation for Religious sent a letter to the president of the National Conference of Catholic Bishops, addressing the widespread changes that had taken place regarding the religious habit. Based on the documents *Perfectae caritatis* and *Evangelica testificatio*, it stated:

> ... religious institutes in their general chapters, may, and in some cases ought to, modify the traditional habit in accord with practical requirements and the needs of hygiene, but they may not abolish it altogether or leave it to the judgement of individual sisters.
>
> The basic criterion to be observed is that the habit prescribed by religious institutes, even as modified and simplified,

should be such that it distinguishes the religious person who wears it.

On the other hand, purely secular clothes, without any recognizable exterior sign, can be permitted, for particular reasons, by the competent superiors to those sisters to whom the use of the religious habit would constitute an impediment or obstacle in the normal exercise of activities which should be undertaken in certain circumstances.

Even in this latter case, the dress of religious women should not depart from the forms of poverty, simplicity, and modesty proper to the religious state. It should always be in some way different from the forms that are clearly secular.

Some sisters, believing that the wearing of the habit remained a matter within their own jurisdiction, resented the Vatican's letter to the National Conference of Catholic Bishops as an indirect interference in their internal community affairs.

The Fallout

Although thousands of nuns across the globe freely embraced new forms of dress during the 1960s and 1970s, those who adopted secular clothing did not do so without negative consequences. The courtesies offered to them in the past, such as store discounts, free bus rides, clergy travel rates, and gratis meals, were no longer offered. Even though many sisters retained their religious wedding bands, their "invisibility" made them vulnerable to unwanted attention from males. They could no longer rely on the somewhat protective nature of the habit in dangerous urban areas. While the meticulous maintenance of starched and folded garb was a thing of the past, nuns were faced with having to choose their own clothing, style their hair, shave their legs, and spend more time on their appearance than was previously necessary. Some found this to be a disadvantage. Most significantly, religious women out of habit experienced tremendous harassment and discrimination, particularly at the parish level and from family members. Laypeople continued to express shock and outrage at the clothing changes, and alumni of Catholic schools and universities where the sisters no longer wore habits complained bitterly, threatening the sisters' financial security.

Nuns often retained their habits for the good of their community or their own personal welfare. Some, however, did so simply because they felt uncomfortable out of the habit. In many cases, women religious pieced together their own makeshift habits. In her memoir, *Changing Habits,* author V. V. Harrison recounts the following conversation with Sister Morgan, a member of the Society of the Sacred Heart:

> I tried getting out of the habit once, but I didn't like it at all. I just looked like a big fat slob. I like beautiful clothes and I knew if I was going to wear beautiful clothes I had to pay for them, and I couldn't take money from the Society to buy the kind of clothes I wanted, so I just went back to the habit and I have been in it ever since. Besides, I want people to know that I am a nun. A lot of people say they don't want that kind of identification. They say when the driver on the bus sees a habit he puts his hand over the fare box so you don't have to pay, and they say how disgraceful, but I say nonsense. I've accepted that many times. After all, we are poor; why wouldn't we accept it?[22]

Yet many sisters felt that in taking control of their own attire they had achieved a tangible liberty. Some described getting out of the habit as the first step in building a personal identity. Sister Francetta, the first nun to be hired by the Women's Job Corps in Washington, D.C., adopted street clothes to work for this antipoverty agency. Dressed in lay attire for the first time, she commented, "The important thing is the individual. I'd rather have one personal confrontation than have a thousand people saying 'Hello, Sister' because of the habit."[23] Some nuns expressed the idea that secular clothing made them feel more "human" and greatly improved relationships with the people whom they served, putting them at their ease. It provided a tremendous psychological boost to those sisters who believed that they had previously always been looked on in stereotypical ways. They felt more feminine and less "androgynous." No longer were they set apart as holy objects, and the new modes of dress symbolized social and personal redefinitions.

In 1963, about the same time that the Second Vatican Council convened, Betty Friedan published her best-seller, *The Feminine Mystique*, and many American women religious became deeply involved with the feminist movement it inspired. Nuns, always examples of strong, independent, and professional women, had been working as hospital administrators and university presidents long before most lay women would have ever been offered these types of opportunities. In 1968 Mary Daly published *The Church and the Second Sex*, which postulated that the Catholic Church was a major oppressor of women. For some sisters, the habit and veil represented the very idea of male dominance, and they compared the clothing to the burka of the Middle East. Feminist scholar Sandra Schneiders, IHM, wrote:

> The implications for the lifestyle of religious were probably more disturbing for the average sister than was the theological revision to which they were related. Perhaps the symbolic lynch pin of the entire movement was the rapid, but wrenching, surrender of the habit which was both the symbol of and implied superiority and uniqueness, and the most effective barrier to the assimilation of religious to the surrounding culture.[24]

In 1969 Sister Margaret Ellen Traxler founded the National Coalition of American Nuns, an organization that is not recognized by the Vatican. She stated that the group formed to "protest any dominion of our institutes by priests, no matter what their hierarchical status. We uphold as inviolable [the] rights of self-determination for religious women."[25] In 1971 the Council of Major Superiors of Women changed its name to the Leadership Conference of Women Religious (LCWR) to reflect its new focus on empowerment for nuns. That same year the organization lost several members to the newly formed *Consortium Perfectae Caritatis* (Association of Perfect Love), a coalition of conservative superiors of orders who proclaimed their intention to remain loyal to tradition. They represented communities that believed that nuns should continue to wear the habit and opposed those that they believed had lost interest in the Vatican's approval. By the end of the 1970s, clothing marked a definitive split among Catholic sisters: Liberal and "progressive" nuns wore secular clothing, and conservative nuns retained the habit. A nun's choice of clothing became a visual barometer of her politics, philosophy, and loyalties—a distinction that in many cases remains to the present day.

CHAPTER NINE

Remnants

*I*n a talk in 1979, Pope John Paul II stated, "People need signs and reminders of God in the modern secular city, which has few reminders of God left. So do not help the trend towards 'taking God off the streets' by adapting secular modes of dress and behavior yourselves!" In 1983 a new Code of Canon Law was issued, which remains in place today. It includes just one canon regarding the habit:

> Canon 669, §1. Religious are to wear the habit of the institute determined according to the norm of proper law as a sign of their consecration and as a testimony of poverty. §2. Clerical religious of an institute which does not have its own habit are to wear clerical dress according to the norm of canon 284.

Canon law expert Elizabeth McDonough, OP, clarifies that the primary function of habit today is to serve as a sign of consecration and witness to poverty. Unlike the previous code, the habit need not necessarily be worn at all times, although the habit guidelines of a congregation are to be determined only by a "competent superior" rather than individuals. Sister Elizabeth also stresses that the veil is not mandated as part of a woman's habit and that the revised ritual for consecration of virgins and the revised ritual for religious profession do not require that a veil be given, although blessings for the ring and the veil still exist for orders that utilize them. As in the past, no distinctions are made between the habit requirements for religious men and women.

Yet by the late 1970s, many Catholic sisters had completely dismissed the notion of wearing the habit. They believed that papal opinion was not necessarily the will of God and that Rome's involvement with their clothing was actually a deeper issue of personal control. More and more religious women, particularly those in America, had become dissatisfied with the patriarchal model of the Church. For some, the habit equaled sexism. It was a uniform of the "good old days" when sisters were expected to be "docile, sexless, cheap labor" and "compliant subjects" of men in power. Even in some older, monastic communities, the habit came to represent a model of religious life they wished to move beyond.

As values changed dramatically within some orders, many sisters left religious life altogether. Some wished to find new rituals and symbols that better expressed their theology and spirituality. Some left because the way of life that they had once held dear had vanished. The number of religious women in the United States declined from 179,954 in 1965 to 115,386 in 1985.[1] Today there are less than 80,000 American Catholic nuns, with a median age of sixty-nine. Women considering religious life today are on the average ten years older than they were thirty years ago.

Some scholars have attributed this dramatic decline to the fact that more professional opportunities have opened up for women who had limited choices thirty years ago. A woman might easily enter the medical and social services professions today without making the personal sacrifices necessary to religious life. Yet in a recent study sociologists Dr. Roger Finke and Dr. Rodney Stark show that prior to the Second Vatican Council, work opportunities for women had been increasing for twenty years with no effect on the steadily increasing numbers of women entering religious life. Dr. Finke and Dr. Stark demonstrated that the changes in religious life itself, as a result of various interpretations of Vatican II's directives, were the main reasons for membership decline and that those orders that maintained their distinct traditions continued to attract new recruits. As director of the American Religion Data Archive, Dr. Finke concludes, "A growing number of scholars have recognized that when religious orders blend in, they fade away."[2]

In a 1999 *National Catholic Reporter* article by Arthur Jones, historian Sister Patricia Byrne observed that total invisibility challenges a nun's clear idea of the structures that support her. Thus, in general, those communities that appear very traditional-looking are growing and those that wear secular clothing are dying out. It is perhaps for this reason that many male and female communities today have retained or have reintroduced the habit. Many new communities forming now typically choose to incorporate some kind of identifiable clothing into their rules. "The habit is back!" observes one contemporary religious brother. New, young religious do not feel their clothing is connected to nostalgic feelings but to a proper interpretation of the documents of Vatican II. New religious candidates are searching for a sense of the mystical and the transcendent—not a return to the past but a rediscovery of the age-old substance and meaning to consecrated life.

"The old Catholic Action movement said to be invisible leaven in the dough, but this has been tried and found wanting. Young people want to be a part of a visible church," observed Father Albert DiIanni, vocation director for the Boston province of the Marist Society, in a 1998 *America* article. Father DiIanni feels that it is important for older religious not to project their needs and values onto the young. In many cases, today's youth are vastly different from the freedom-seeking young people of the 1960s. Today's teens are looking for security and clearly delineated models of religious life. They do not feel the same antagonism toward the Church as did their parents, having no memories of a "repressive" Church. "Generation X's tastes seem more in line with that of our grandparents," says Father DiIanni. "It is difficult for persons over forty-five to realize that the revolution is over. . . . The statue of the Blessed Virgin Mary at Boston College is constantly adorned with flowers. At Georgetown, a group of students petitioned the Jesuits in 1996 to restore a crucifix in every room."[3]

Many young people today gravitate to visual symbols, including the habit. A recent study done for the LCWR by Dr. Dean Hoge showed that young people today saw no objections to wearing the habit. The vocations directors at many women's religious orders report that one of the first questions asked of them is "Do you wear a habit?" Yet other women's religious communities discount the appeal of the habit to modern youth, believing it to be a superficial and idyllic fascination. They try to attract new recruits by presenting a view of religious life they feel will be the most legitimately appealing. The website of the Ursulines of Youngstown states:

> If you think an Ursuline is someone who hides inside the dark folds of a convent and habit, think again. We are a dynamic group of women who see the needs of today's society and have dared to do something about them. We have real lives and real jobs. We are educators, social workers, health care professionals and administrators. And we do all the things you like to do—see movies, take classes, play sports. As Ursulines, we continually search for ways to grow personally and spiritually.

The website of the IHM Congregation in Scranton, Pennsylvania, states: "Now, rather than rely on our external appearance, we challenge ourselves to let what we say, what we do, what we stand for and what we model by our choices give witness to who we are as women religious." Many orders hope that the focus of their community—rather than the "look"—will attract professional candidates who are serious about making a lifelong commitment. Even some orders considered "conservative" have recently elected to abandon habits for secular clothes to define more accurately their roles in the community. In 1990 the Sisters of Notre Dame of Chardon, Ohio, asked the Consumer

Sciences Department at Ohio State University to present workshops to their sisters to assist their clothing transformation. In 1997 the Daughters of Charity of St. Vincent de Paul chose to eliminate their habits in favor of street clothes. The sisters indicated their change came from the spirit of simplicity and wishing to be respectful of the ordinary people in the areas they served. Sister Genevieve Keusenkothen comments, "This does not mean that we hide who we are (which seems to be impossible). I find repeatedly that people just know we are sisters. We do wear an emblem that signifies our membership in the Vincentian family, either as a pendant or a lapel pin."

Nonetheless, it seems that those institutes retaining the greatest numbers and experiencing the greatest growth are those that embrace traditional forms of dress. A Georgetown University study shows that in 1993, "traditional" orders in the United States had more women in formation than "progressive" orders.[4] Many religious and lay Catholics believe that the mainline congregations would be able to gain more recruits if they returned to the habit and other traditional forms of religious life. Conservative orders receive a boost from the very popular television celebrity Mother Angelica, founding director of cable station Eternal Word Television Network (EWTN). Mother Angelica returned to wearing the traditional habit within the last decade and is regarded as the Oprah Winfrey of the Catholic media. When Mother Angelica hosts a traditional religious community on her show, it experiences a dramatic boost in inquiries afterward. A Daughter of St. Paul sister recently recalled, "Seated around Mother Angelica were several sisters of different religious orders. And sitting on the right side of Mother Angelica was a sister wearing a blue habit. This caught my eye because blue is one of my favorite colors, plus her habit was very simple."[5]

Vocations are booming in Africa, Indonesia, Latin America, and India among conservative orders whose rule includes the habit. Some sisters from "progressive" orders attribute this phenomenon to the opportunities for education and a better way of life offered. However, modern, well-educated professional women in the United States follow the same path. New York's late John Cardinal O'Connor founded the Sisters of Life in 1991 to foster the protection of human life. Sisters pray to end abortion and staff crisis pregnancy centers. Their community includes a former air force nurse, a former business owner, and a former medical student. Mother Superior Agnes Donovan was a professor of psychology at Columbia University. Between 100 and 125 potential candidates visit the Sisters of Life each year. Their habit is dark blue and white, loosely modeled after the Dominican forms. Standing out starkly in their Bronx, New York, neighborhood, the sisters report that people flock to them, telling their problems or begging for prayers. No sister can recall ever being ridiculed or receiving negative feedback. On the contrary, the nuns view this type of recognition as a privilege that would not be possible without the habit. Sister Mary Elizabeth also points out that their inviting habit is an eschatological sign of Christ's love and a positive symbol of God, who is "all beautiful."

Today many sisters report receiving the express thanks from laypeople when they appear in their habits in public. These people feel the habit serves as a radical statement of belief in a world that seeks signs. Sister Antoinette, of a Salesian order of teaching nuns in Kansas, told the *Kansas City Star*, "I am a sister for twenty-two years, and I have never found that a young person wouldn't be able to relate. We wear our habit all the time—to work, to play with the kids, to run around. You just put it in the washing machine. The next day we're ready." Yet other sisters continue to express a different perspective. "For every time the habit offered positive witness, I think there was a matching occasion when it scared people away, or caused them to put the habit-wearer onto some kind of pedestal, and the difference between a pedestal and a shelf has always escaped me," remembers Sister Margaret Campbell, SNMJ.

In 1995 Pope John Paul II canonically approved a new American association, the Council of Major Superiors of Women Religious (CMSWR). It had been founded in 1992 as an alternative to the

Leadership Conference of Women Religious, whose members generally do not wear a habit. The CMSWR is made up of communities that share a common view of religious life, which includes the wearing of religious dress. In 1993, approximately 81 percent of women's religious institutes were members of the LCWR and 12 percent belonged to the CMSWR, with 4 percent belonging to both and 7 percent belonging to neither.[6] The existence of these two associations clearly demonstrates the differences in attitudes regarding dress among women religious today. It is a clash that continues to spark painful debate among sisters, clergy, and laity, and one that is likely to continue in the future. One sister remarks, "It is amazing that discussion about the habit is so relatable to having a root canal."

Some sisters regret that clothing issues have divided Catholic nuns into an "us" versus "them" situation. Most are generous in speaking about one another and prefer to focus their time and attention on their apostolates. Yet the mission of clearly defining a community's identity remains crucial to its survival. The habit represents stability and touches something within the human psyche that no other symbol seems able to match. Thousands of sisters labor every day, reaching out to poor families, caring for prostitutes with AIDS, ministering to death-row prisoners, and changing the world for the better. Tomorrow Sister Mary Catharine of Jesus, OP, will dress for a day of prayer and labor in her floor-length tunic, flowing veil, and sandals. School Sister of St. Francis Clare Korte will wear a lab coat to teach biology at the University of Minnesota in Winona. And Sister Gail Miller, Sisters of the Earth, will wear a uniform denim dress while working with her community to foster sustainable building design and alternative energy use. Many sisters today wear business suits, overalls, or surgical scrubs—whatever makes sense for their work.

Still, the world will continue to visualize Catholic nuns in terms of the habit. Those in secular dress often seem "invisible" in spite of their continued commitment to their vows of chastity, poverty, and obedience. Mark Twain once said, "There is no power without clothes. It is the power that governs the human race." Perhaps it is for this reason the habit has lasted. Brother Anthony Luke of Adoramus House (*nuns habits.com*) is swamped with orders for official habits from everyone from legitimate Catholic religious to Broadway producers and museums in search of his hand-tailored creations. The Cholewa brothers of Blessings Expressions of Faith do a brisk business selling nun dolls dressed in meticulously reproduced habits. We do not seem able to part with the rituals and symbols of the habit, which has been a part of our civilization for two thousand years. Like the priest's vestments at Mass, the habit perhaps becomes a portal from the earthly world to the spiritual, giving us a visible opportunity to partake in the eternal.

Appendix and Glossary of Church Terms

In describing the religious habit, some general terms are used which may not be familiar to the reader. Habit refers to the ensemble of clothing and accessories that makes up one's religious dress. It can also mean specifically the robelike tunic or dress that is the main garment worn over the body. The veil is the long cloth worn on the top of the head, extending down the back. Some veils are designed to be pulled forward over the face, and other veils are designed to be worn as thin linings beneath heavier veils. The veil is usually attached to a cap underneath, or coif, which is a close-fitting cloth headpiece that conforms to the shape of the skull and often ties under the chin. A wimple or guimpe is the fabric piece that covers the neck and chest, and sometimes extended over the chin. A bandeau is the piece that stretches across the forehead, often attached at the ears behind the veil. A scapular is a long apronlike garment that is worn over the tunic and which extends down both the front and back of the tunic. A cincture is a belt worn around the waist of the tunic, and a Rosary is a string of prayer beads and other objects often attached to the cincture and worn at the side. A cappa, cape, or mantle refers to a cloak worn over the tunic.

Photographs of Historic Habits circa 1958

CONGREGATION OF THE
ASSUMPTION

DAUGHTERS OF CHARITY OF
ST. VIINCENT DE PAUL

Founded in Paris, 1888. The religious wore a purple habit with a white woolen cross, a purple cincture, and a white woolen veil. A white cloak was worn in choir and on special feast days.

Founded in Paris, 1633. The garb of the Sister of Charity was that of the peasant girl of the time. Once so inconspicuous in the streets of Paris, the white cornette and blue gown of the Sister of Charity was easily identified, even in a convention hall crowded with a thousand nuns of various orders.

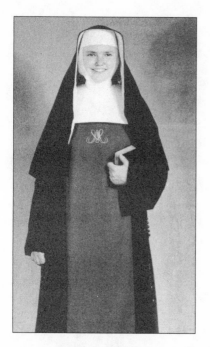

DAUGHTERS OF
MARY AND JOSEPH

*Founded in Belgium, 1817. The sisters
wore a black robe and veil, headdress and
guimpe of white linen, and scapular and
belt of Our Lady's blue. On the veil and
on the front of the scapular was
embroidered the monogram of their
heavenly patroness, A.M. (Ave Maria).*

DAUGHTERS OF WISDOM

*Founded in France, 1703. The habit was
made of coarse gray serge. A large linen
handkerchief covered the shoulders, and a
starched white linen headdress was worn in
lieu of a veil. A large ebony crucifix was
worn on the breast and a Rosary hung at
the side, conspicuous against the gray of the
dress.*

FRANCISCAN SISTERS OF
BLESSED KUNEGUNDA

*Founded in Chicago, 1894. The professed
wore a brown woolen habit, with a white
guimpe, coif, brow band, cornet, cord, black
veil, crucifix, and Franciscan crown
Rosary.*

LITTLE SISTERS OF THE POOR

*Founded in France, 1839. The habit of
the Little Sister consisted of a black robe
with a kerchief and apron; the black mantle
was worn in the chapel and when
traveling. The headdress was a plain white
bonnet with a forehead band symbolic of
obedience.*

MARYKNOLL SISTERS

Founded in New York, 1912. The habit consisted of a black veil, a gray tunic and scapular with a waist-length cape. The Miraculous Medal hung by a chain around the neck; the Rosary was of Job's tears.

MISSIONARY SERVANTS OF THE MOST BLESSED TRINITY

Founded in Brooklyn, New York, 1909. Sister wore black dress, simply tailored with a cincture having three tabs signifying the vows of poverty, chastity, and obedience; black buttons; white collar and cuffs. A black hat and coat were worn when visiting.

OBLATE SISTERS OF PROVIDENCE

Founded Baltimore, Maryland, 1829. After six months the postulant received the habit, which consisted of a black serge garment, black apron and cape, a white guimpe, coif, headband, and white veil. Professed sisters wore a black veil.

ORDER OF ST. URSULA

Founded in Brescia, Italy, 1535. The sisters of the Roman Union wore a black habit and veil fastened by a cincture; white was worn in the tropics. The Ursulines of Paris wore a black habit with a long trailing church mantle and a leather cincture of St. Augustine.

POOR HANDMAIDS
OF JESUS CHRIST

SISTER OF THE
ORDER OF MERCY

*Founded in Dernbach, Germany, 1851.
The habit was black serge, pleated, with a
black cincture around the waist from which
is suspended a large Rosary. The black veil
is pinned to a starched white coronet that
buttons below the chin. A white linen
collar completed the ensemble.*

*Founded in Dublin, Ireland, 1831. The
habit was black wool, plaited at the waist;
a cincture of black leather, a black veil, and
a silver ring completed the habit of the
professed Mercy sister.*

SISTERS OF THE
GOOD SHEPHERD

SISTERS OF BON SECOURS

Founded in France, 1641. The habit of the Sisters of the Good Shepherd was white with a blue girdle. Hanging from the neck and displayed in front was a large silver heart. On one side of it was engraved the figure of Jesus the Good Shepherd and on the other, the Blessed Mother.

Founded in Paris, 1824. The religious habit was of black serge, with a black veil, white fichu, white fluted cap, and white cuffs. When on duty with the sick the sisters wore white.

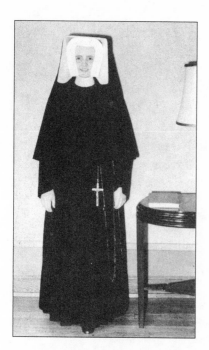

SISTERS OF CHARITY OF
THE BLESSED VIRGIN MARY

SISTERS OF CHARITY OF
THE INCARNATE WORD

Founded in Philadelphia, 1833. The black serge habit included a cape with a white collar, a pleated skirt and apron, a cincture with Rosary and crucifix attached, a white cap and hood, and a black veil.

Founded in France, 1625. The holy habit was black; the headdress was of white linen with a black veil. On the front of the scapular, the symbol of the Incarnate Word was embroidered with red silk.

SISTERS OF CHARITY,
"GREY NUNS OF MONTREAL"

Founded in Montreal, Canada, 1738. The simple garb of the Grey Nuns consisted of a gray habit and black headdress. They also wore a silver cross.

SISTERS OF CHARITY

Founded in Emmitsburg, Maryland, 1835. The dress was the black cap of Mother Seton with an inner white cap; a simply made black habit with a white collar and white inner sleeves; black apron and cape.

SISTERS OF CHRISTIAN CHARITY

Founded in Paderborn, Germany, 1849. The sisters' habit consisted of a long simple black dress, cape, and apron, a black veil, and mantle. The collar, cuffs, and coif were white linen.

SISTERS OF LORETTO AT THE FOOT OF THE CROSS

Founded in Cologne, France, 1849. A Sister of Loretto wore a simple black wool dress, a black veil over a shaped white lining, a white collar, a black leather cincture, and a Seven Dolors Rosary.

SISTERS OF SOCIAL SERVICE

SISTERS OF ST. BASIL THE GREAT

Founded in Budapest, Hungary, 1908. The sisters wore a simple gray uniform and the emblem of the Society, a silver medal bearing the dove, the symbol of the Holy Spirit. For street wear the uniform was completed by a narrow-brimmed hat of matching color, from which dropped a soft gray veil. Indoors the head was left uncovered.

Founded in Uniontown, Pennsylvania, 1921. The sisters wore a black habit and scapular, with a black girdle (belt) and veil, a white wimple, and a Rosary. The three folds at the bottom of the habit, sleeves, and wimple denoted the three vows of poverty, chastity, and obedience.

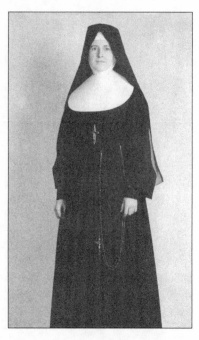

SISTERS OF ST. CASIMIR

SISTERS OF ST. JOSEPH

Founded in Pennsylvania, 1907. The professed sister wore a black veil, black serge habit, and black scapular. In honor of Our Lady, she also wore a Rosary at her right side and a blue cord at her left. A large white collar, a silver crucifix, and a gold ring completed her outfit.

Founded in Velay, France, 1650. The habit was made of black material with full skirt and sleeves, a soft black veil, and a guimpe and cornet of white material.

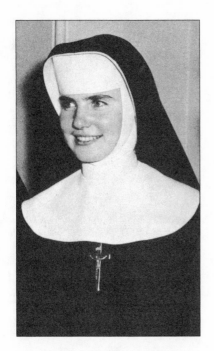

SISTERS OF THE BLESSED
SACRAMENT FOR INDIANS AND
COLORED PEOPLE

*Founded in Philadelphia, Pennsylvania,
1891. The sisters wore a black habit and
scapular with an ebony crucifix, a white
Franciscan cord, and a large Rosary. The
veil was black. In adoration of the Blessed
Sacrament and in processions, the sisters
wore a white church cloak.*

SISTERS OF THE HOLY CROSS

*Founded in LeMans, France, 1843. The
black habit of the sisters was characterized
by the Rosary of the Seven Dolors worn at
their right side, while a blue cord in honor
of Mary was worn at the left. A silver
heart bearing the image of Our Lady of
Sorrows, the patroness and model of the
sisters, was suspended from a circular
collar. The headdress was a fluted cap that
evolved from that of French peasants of the
province where the community was
founded.*

SISTERS OF THE HOLY FAMILY

Founded in San Francisco, California, 1872. The habit, veil, and cape of the professed sister were of black serge. The collar, guimpe, headband, and bonnet were of white linen. A Rosary of six decades in honor of St. Bridget, a seven-knotted cincture of St. Joseph, a crucifix, and a gold ring completed the religious garb.

SISTERS OF THE THIRD ORDER OF ST. DOMINIC OF THE HOLY CROSS

Originally founded in 1206 in Prioulle, France, the Holy Cross convent branch emerged later in the thirteenth century in Ratisbon, Germany. The American branch originated in 1853. The professed religious of the Dominican order wore a white habit, a black mantle, and a black veil lined with white.

SISTERS, SERVANTS OF THE
IMMACULATE HEART OF MARY

*Founded in Monroe, Michigan, 1845. The
habit was serge, blue in honor of the
Immaculate Conception.*

SOCIETY OF THE SACRED HEART

*Founded in Paris, France, 1800. The
habit was a simple black dress with a black
cape. A long black veil was worn over a
white cap with a fluted border. A Rosary, a
silver cross, and a plain ring completed the
habit.*

Glossary of Church Terms

Adapted from *Glossary of Church Terms,* Copyright © 2001, United States Conference of Catholic Bishops, Inc. Washington, D.C. Used with permission. All rights reserved. No part of this document may be reproduced in any way without permission in writing from the copyright holder.

absolution: Act by which a priest, acting as the agent of Christ, grants forgiveness of sins in the Sacrament of Penance.

acolyte: One who assists in the celebration (i.e., carrying candles, holding the pope's staff miter, etc.).

Adoration of the Blessed Sacrament: Prayer to Christ, who is recognized as being truly present in the Sacrament, which is displayed for the people.

altar: A table on which the sacrifice of the Mass is offered. It is the center of importance in the place where the Mass is celebrated. Also called the Table of the Lord.

apostle, apostolic, disciple: Literally "one sent." Normally this refers to the twelve men chosen by Christ to be the bearers of His teachings to the world. The term "apostolic" generally refers back to the twelve apostles. In the Church it characterizes certain documents, appointments, or structures initiated by the pope or the Holy See. Disciple is one who follows the teachings of Jesus.

apostolate: The ministry or work of an apostle. In Catholic usage, a term covering all kinds and areas of work and endeavor for the service of God and the Church and the good of people.

archbishop: Title given automatically to bishops who govern archdioceses.

archdiocese: The chief diocese of an ecclesiastical province.

basilica: A church to which special privileges are attached. It is a title of honor given to various kinds of churches.

beatification: Final step toward canonization of a saint.

bishops: The chief priest of a diocese. Bishops are responsible for the pastoral care of their dioceses. In addition, bishops have a responsibility to act in counsel with other bishops to guide the Church.

Blessed Sacrament: The Eucharist, the Body and Blood of Christ, whether at the Mass or reserved in a special place in the Church.

Book of Gospels: The book that contains the Gospel texts, from which the priest or deacon proclaims the Gospel of the day.

brother: A man who is a member of a religious order but is not ordained or studying for the priesthood.

canon law: The codified body of general laws governing the Church.

canon: Greek for rule, norm, standard, measure. Designates the Canon of Sacred Scripture, the list of books recognized by the Church as inspired by the Holy Spirit.

canonization: A declaration by the pope that a person who died a martyr or practiced Christian virtue to a heroic degree is in heaven and is worthy of honor and imitation by the faithful. Verification of miracles is required for canonization (except for martyrs).

cardinal: Cardinals are appointed by the pope and constitute a kind of senate of the Church, and aid the pope as his chief counselors.

cassock: A nonliturgical, full-length, close-fitting robe for use by priests and other clerics under liturgical vestments; usually black for priests, purple for bishops and other prelates, red for cardinals, white for the pope.

catechetics: From the Greek meaning "to sound forth," it is the procedure for teaching religion.

cathedral: The major Church in an archdiocese or diocese. It is the seat of the local Ordinary.

Catholic: Greek word for "universal." First used in the title "Catholic Church" in a letter written by St. Ignatius of Antioch to the Christians of Smyrna about A.D. 107.

celebrant: The one who presides at the celebration of the Eucharist.

charism: Gift or grace given by God to persons for the good of others and the Church.

charismatic: Person who believes God endowed him or her with gifts or graces.

Christ: The title of Jesus, derived from the Greek translation of the Hebrew term "Messiah," meaning "the Anointed of God."

Church: The universal Church that is spread throughout the world; the local Church is that of a particular locality, such as a diocese. The Church embraces all its members—on earth, in heaven, in purgatory.

clergy: Collective term referring to male persons who administer the rites of the Church through Holy Orders.

cloister: Part of a convent or monastery reserved for use by members of the institute.

College of Cardinals: Made up of the cardinals of the Church, who advise the pope, assist in the central administration of the Church, head the various curial offices and congregations, administer the Holy See during a vacancy, and elect a new pope.

Conference of Major Superiors of Men (CMSM): Organization of major superiors representing communities of men religious in the United States.

confession: Only part of the Sacrament of Penance or reconciliation, not a term for the sacrament.

confirmation: One of the three sacraments of initiation, along with baptism and Eucharist.

contemplative nun: A religious woman who devotes her entire life in the cloister to prayer and reflection.

convent: In common usage, the term refers to a house of women religious.

Council of Major Superiors of Women Religious (CMSWR): Organization of major superiors approved by the Holy See for the purpose of assisting the individual institutes of members, transacting common business, and fostering suitable coordination and cooperation with the conferences of bishops and also with individual bishops.

crosier (pastoral staff): The staff that a bishop carries when he presides at the liturgy.

cross, crucifix: An object is a crucifix only if it depicts Christ on a cross; otherwise it is a cross.

cult: In generic use, "cult" denotes any act or system of veneration or worship.

dalmatic: The vestment the deacon wears over the alb on solemn occasions.

deacon: An ordained minister who assists the Celebrant at the Liturgy of the Word and at the altar for the Liturgy of the Eucharist.

deacons, diaconate: The diaconate is the first order or grade in ordained ministry. Any man who is to be ordained to the priesthood must first be ordained as a transitional deacon. Deacons serve in the ministry of liturgy, of the word, and of charity. The permanent diaconate is for men who do not plan to become ordained priests. The program is open to both married and unmarried men.

dean, vicar: The title of a priest appointed by the bishop to aid him in administering the parishes in a certain vicinity, called a "deanery." The function of a dean involves promotion, coordination, and supervision of the common pastoral activity within the deanery or vicariate.

diocese: A particular church; a fully organized ecclesiastical jurisdiction under the pastoral direction of a bishop as local ordinary.

dispensation: An exemption from Church law.

Eastern-rite (Oriental) Church: Term used to describe the Catholic

Churches that developed in Eastern Europe, Asia, and Africa. They have their own distinctive liturgical and organizational systems. Each is considered equal to the Latin rite within the Church.

ecclesiastical: Refers to official structures or legal and organizational aspects of the church.

encyclical: A pastoral letter addressed by the pope to the whole Church.

episcopal: Refers to a bishop or groups of bishops as a form of church government, in which bishops have authority.

excommunication: A penalty of censure by which a baptized person is excluded from the communion of the faithful for committing and remaining obstinate in certain serious offenses specified in canon law. Even though excommunicated, a person still is responsible for fulfilling the normal obligations of a Catholic.

God: The infinitely perfect Supreme Being, uncaused and absolutely self-sufficient, eternal, the Creator and final end of all things. The one God subsists in three equal Persons, the Father and the Son and the Holy Spirit.

grace: A free gift of God to human beings, grace is a created sharing in the life of God. It is given through the merits of Christ and is communicated by the Holy Spirit. It is necessary for salvation.

hierarchy: In general, the term refers to the ordered body of clergy, divided into bishops, priests, and deacons. In Catholic practice, the term refers to the bishops of the world or of a particular region.

holidays, Holy Days of Obligation: Feasts in Latin-rite churches on which Catholics are required to assist at Mass. In the United States these are: Christmas (the Nativity of Jesus); January 1 (Mary Mother of God); Ascension of the Lord forty days after Easter; August 15 (Assumption of the Blessed Virgin Mary); November 1 (All Saints' Day); and December 8, Immaculate Conception (of the Blessed Virgin Mary). Outside the United States, variations of Holy Days may occur.

Holy Communion: After saying a preparatory prayer, the celebrant (or other designated ministers) gives communion (the consecrated bread and wine) to himself and the other ministers at the altar, and then communion is distributed to the congregation.

Holy See: (1) The diocese of the pope, Rome. (2) The pope himself or the various officials and bodies of the Church's central administration—the Roman Curia—that act in the name and by authority of the pope.

homily: The homily (sermon) is a reflection by the celebrant or other ministers on the Scripture readings and the application of the texts to the assembled community.

Host, the Sacred: The bread under whose appearances Christ is and remains present in a unique manner after the consecration of the Mass.

IHS: In Greek, the first three letters of the name of Jesus.

Immaculate Conception: Catholic dogma concerning Mary and the name of a feast in her honor celebrated December 8. It refers to the Catholic belief that Mary was without sin from the moment she was conceived.

incense: A material that produces a fragrant odor when burned and is used as a symbol of the Church's offering and prayer going up to God.

indulgence: The remission before God of the temporal punishment due for sins already forgiven.

intercessions: A series of prayers for the Church, the world, the pope, clergy and laity, and the dead.

Jesus: The name of Jesus, meaning "Savior" in Christian usage, derived from the Aramaic and Hebrew Yeshua and Joshua, meaning "Yahweh is salvation."

layman, woman, person: Any Church member who is neither ordained nor a member of a religious order. When the Second Vatican Council spoke of the laity, it used the term in this more common meaning.

Leadership Conference of Women Religious (LCWR): Organization of major superiors, who represent more than 90 percent of the active women religious in the United States.

Liturgy of the Hours: The preferred term in the Latin rite for the official liturgical prayers sanctifying the parts of each day.

liturgy: The public prayer of the Church.

Lord's Prayer: The prayer of petition for both daily food (which for Christians means also the Eucharistic bread) and the forgiveness of sins.

magisterium: The official teaching office of the Church.

Mary: The central point of the theology of Mary is that she is the Mother of God. From apostolic times, tradition, the Church, and the faithful have accorded to Mary the highest forms of veneration. She is celebrated in feasts throughout the year and in devotions such as the Rosary and litany and is hailed the patroness of many countries, including the United States.

Mass: The common name for the Eucharistic liturgy of the Catholic Church.

matrimony: The Roman, Orthodox, and Old Catholic churches consider matrimony a sacrament, referred to as the Sacrament of Matrimony. This is a marriage contract between baptized persons.

miracles, apparitions: Generally, "miracle" is used to refer to physical phenomena that defy natural explanation, such as medically unexplainable cures. "Apparition" refers to a supernatural manifestation of God, an angel, or a saint to an individual or a group of individuals.

mitre: A headdress worn at some liturgical functions by bishops, abbots, and, in certain cases, other ecclesiastics.

monastery: An autonomous community house of a religious order, which may or may not be a monastic order. The term is used more specifically to refer to a community house of men or women religious in which they lead a contemplative life separate from the world.

monk, friar: A man who belongs to one of the monastic orders in the church, such as Basilians, Benedictines, Cistercians, and Carthusians.

monsignor: An honorary ecclesiastical title granted by the pope to some diocesan priests. In the United States, the title is given to the vicar general of a diocese. In Europe, the title is also given to bishops.

nun: (1) Strictly, a member of a religious order of women with solemn vows; (2) in general, all women religious, even those in simple vows who are more properly called sisters.

ordain, ordination: The proper terms in Catholic usage for references to the conferral of the Sacrament of Holy Orders on a deacon, priest, or bishop.

order, congregation, society: "Religious orders" is a title loosely applied to all religious groups of men and women. "Society" is a body of clerics, regular or secular, organized the purpose of performing an apostolic work. "Congregation" is any group bound together by common rules.

pallium: Special stole made of lamb's wool worn over the chasuble by the pope and archbishops; it signifies communion of archbishops with the Holy See.

papal infallibility: The end result of divine assistance given the pope, wherefore he is prevented from the possibility and liability of error in teachings on faith or morals.

parish: A specific community of the Christian faithful within a diocese, which has its own church building, under the authority of a pastor who is responsible for providing them with ministerial service. Most parishes are formed on a geographic basis, but they may be formed along national or ethnic lines.

pastor: A priest in charge of a parish or congregation. He is responsible for administering the sacraments, instructing the congregation in the doctrine of the Church, and other services to the people of the parish.

pontiff, pontifical: Used as an alternative form of reference to the pope. "Pontifical" has to do with the pope.

prayer: The raising of the mind and heart to God in adoration, thanksgiving, reparation, and petition. The official prayer of the Church as a worshipping community is called liturgy.

primacy: "Papal primacy" refers to the pope's authority over the whole Church.

proselytize: To bring one to another's viewpoint, whether in religion or other areas.

province: (1) A territory comprising one archdiocese called the metropolitan see and one or more dioceses called suffragan sees. The head of an archdiocese, an archbishop, has metropolitan rights and responsibilities over the province. (2) A division of a religious order under the jurisdiction of a provincial superior.

purgatory: The state or condition in which those who have died in the state of grace, but with some attachment to sin, suffer for a time as they are being purified before they are admitted to the glory and happiness of heaven.

relics: The physical remains and effects of saints, which are considered worthy of veneration inasmuch as they are representative of persons in glory with God.

retreat: A period of time spent in meditation and religious exercise. Retreats may take various forms, from traditional closed forms, to open retreats that do not disengage the participants from day-to-day life. Both clergy and laypeople of all ages participate in retreats. Houses and centers providing facilities for retreats are retreat houses.

Roman Curia: The official collective name for the administrative agencies and courts, and their officials, that assist the pope in governing the Church. Members are appointed and granted authority by the pope.

Rome, diocese of: The City of Rome is the diocese of the pope, as the bishop of Rome.

Rosary: A prayer of meditation primarily on events in the lives of Mary and Jesus, repeating the Our Father and Hail Mary. It is generally said on a physical circlet of beads.

sanctuary: That part of the church where the altar is located.

Second Vatican Council: A major meeting of the bishops of the world convened by Pope John XXIII to bring about a renewal of the Church for the second half of the twentieth century. It ran from 1962 to 1965 and produced important documents in liturgy, ecumenism, communications, and other areas.

secular institutes: Societies of men and women living in the world who dedicate themselves to observe the evangelical counsels and to carry on apostolic works suitable to their talents and opportunities in every day life.

see: Another name for diocese or archdiocese.

seminary: An educational institutional for men preparing for Holy Orders.

shrine: Erected to encourage private devotions to a saint, it usually contains a picture, statue, or other religious feature capable of inspiring devotions.

Sign of the Cross: A sign, ceremonial gesture, or movement in the form of a cross by which a person confesses faith in the Holy Trinity and Christ, and intercedes for the blessing of himself, other persons, and things.

sister: In popular speech, any woman religious. Strictly, the title applies to those women religious belonging to institutes whose members never professed solemn vows; most of these institutes were established during and since the nineteenth century.

sodality: A group of laity established for the promotion of Christian life and worship or some other religious purpose.

Stations of the Cross: Also known as the Way of the Cross, this devotion to the suffering of Christ consist of prayers and meditations on fourteen occurrences experienced by Christ on His way to His crucifixion. Each of these occurrences is represented by a cross. This devotion can be done individually, or in groups with one person leading the prayers and moving from cross to cross.

stole: The vestment worn around the neck by all ordained ministers. For priests, bishops, and the pope, it hangs down in front (under the chasuble); deacons wear it over their left shoulder crossed and fastened at the right side.

superior: The head of a religious order or congregation. He or she may be the head of a province or an individual house.

surplice: A loose, flowing vestment of white fabric with wide sleeves. For some functions it is interchangeable with an alb.

synod: A gathering of designated officials and representatives of a church, with legislative and policymaking powers.

tabernacle: Place in the Church where the Eucharist or sacred species is reserved.

theology: The study of God and religion, deriving from and based on the data of divine Revelation, organized and systematized according to some kind of scientific method.

tribunal: A tribunal (court) is the name given to the person or persons who exercise the Church's judicial powers.

United States Conference of Catholic Bishops (USCCB): Episcopal conference of U.S. bishops. The membership is comprised of diocesan bishops and their auxiliary bishops. The conference decides matters of ecclesiastical law and issues policy statements on political and social issues.

Vespers: A portion of the Church's divine office, the daily public prayer encouraged for religious and laity. Also called Evening Prayer.

vestment: The vesture the ministers wear.

vow: A promise made to God with sufficient knowledge and freedom, which has as its object a moral good that is possible and better than its voluntary omission.

Notes

CHAPTER ONE: ENIGMA

1. Mary Gordon, "Women of God," *Atlantic Monthly* (January 2002), 57–88.

2. Rebecca Sullivan, "Breaking Habits: Gender, Class and the Sacred in the Dress of Women Religious," in *Consuming Fashion: Adorning the Transnational Body*. Edited by Anne Brydon and Sandra Niessen (Oxford and New York: Berg, 1998), 109.

3. Carole Garibaldi Rogers, *Poverty, Chastity, and Change: Lives of Contemporary Nuns* (New York: Twayne Publishers, 1996), xx.

4. Jessica Matthews, "An Army of Brides" [online]. Unpublished conference paper. Popular Cultural Association Meeting, Albuquerque, NM, February 27, 1999. Available on the World Wide Web at: *http://www. geocities.com/Wellesley/1114/jmatthews.htm* (December 2002).

5. "Archive of the Catholic League's Annual Reports on Anti-Catholicism" [online]. Available on the World Wide Web at: *http://catholicleague.otg/ archive_of_annualreports.htm* (1994–2001).

6. "The Singing Nun" [online]. Available on the World Wide Web at: *http://www.swinginchicks.com/singing_nun.htm* (December 2002).

7. Arthur Jones, "Nuns Renew Vows" [online]. *National Catholic Reporter* (March 5, 1999). Available on the World Wide Web at: *http://natcath. otg/NCR_Online/archives/030599/030599a.htm.*

8. Elizabeth Ann Murphy, "Where Do Mass Media Images of Priesthood

and Religious Life Come From?" *Horizon* (Spring 1995), 3–7; and Elizabeth Ann Murphy, "Sisters and Cigarettes: Icons of Popular Culture," *LCWR Occasional Papers* (Summer 2000), 3–7.

9. Feister, John Bookser. "Sister Helen Prejean: The Real Woman Behind *Dead Man Walking*" [online]. *St. Anthony Messenger* (April 1996). Available on the World Wide Web at: *http://www.americancatholic.org/Messenger/April1996/feature1asap.*

CHAPTER TWO: TRADITION

1. Little Company of Mary, Province of the Holy Spirit, Hurtsville, BC, NSW, Australia.

2. Adorers of the Precious Blood of Christ, Wichita, KS.

3. Congregation of Sisters, Servants of the Immaculate Heart of Mary, Scranton, PA.

4. Franciscan Sisters of Mary Immaculate, Amarillo, TX.

5. Sullivan, "Breaking Habits," 124.

6. Information on the Maryknoll habit found on pp. 18–22 in the text from Maryknoll Mission, Maryknoll, NY.

7. Dominican Nuns, Monastery of Our Lady of the Rosary, Summit, NJ.

8. Jo Ann Kay McNamara, *Sisters in Arms: Catholic Nuns Through Two Millennia* (Cambridge, MA: Harvard University Press, 1996), 149.

9. Sullivan, "Breaking Habits," 114.

10. Marcelle Bernstein, *The Nuns* (Philadelphia and New York: J. B. Lippincott, 1976), 91.

11. Sisters of the Holy Cross, Notre Dame, IN.

12. Margaret Susan Thompson, "Sisterhood and Power: Class, Culture, and Ethnicity in the American Convent," *Colby Library Quarterly* (September 25, 1989), 149–75.

13. Bernstein, *The Nuns*, 243–45.

14. Sisters of the Holy Cross, Notre Dame, IN.

15. Information on nun dolls found on pp. 33–34 of the text is derived from unpublished research by Judith Swarbrick, Preston, England.

16. Sullivan, "Breaking Habits," 119.

17. Bernstein, *The Nuns*, 242.

18. Adorers of the Blood of Christ, Wichita, KS.

19. Ibid.

20. Dominican Sisters of Edmunds, WA.

21. Sullivan, "Breaking Habits," 119.

22. Sisters of Providence, Seattle, WA.

CHAPTER THREE: HOLINESS

1. Bernstein, *The Nuns*, 257.

2. Sister Maria Boulding, "Background to a Theology of the Monastic Habit." *Downside Review* 98, no. 331 (April 1980), 110–13. Discussion about clothing in Jewish culture on pp. 42–43 of the text draws from this article.

3. Janet Mayo, *A History of Ecclesiastical Dress* (New York: Holmes & Meier Publishers, 1984), 11.

4. Rodney Stark, *The Rise of Christianity: A Sociologist Reconsiders History* (Princeton, NJ: Princeton University Press, 1996), 33–107.

5. Ruth A. Tucker and Walter L. Liefeld, *Daughters of the Church: Women and Ministry from New Testament Times to the Present* (Grand Rapids, MI: Academie Books, 1987), 47–62. Information about Christ and women in this section draws upon many points from Tucker and Liefeld. The Sayers quote featured on p. 48 of the text is from her work *Are Women Human?* (Grand Rapids, MI: William R. Eerdmans Publishing, 1971).

6. Desiree G. Koslin, "The Dress of Monastic and Religious Women as Seen in Art from the Early Middle Ages to the Reformation," Ph.D. diss. (New York University, 1999), 198.

7. Elizabeth Abbott, *A History of Celibacy: From Athena to Elizabeth I, Leonardo da Vinci, Florence Nightingale, Gandhi, & Cher* (New York: Scribner, 1999), 36–41.

8. Koslin, "The Dress of Monastic," 49–50.

9. Elizabeth Schüssler Fiorenza, *In Memory of Her: A Feminist Theological Reconstruction of Christian Origins* (New York: Crossroad Publishing Company, 1983), 228.

10. Susan Michelman, "Breaking Habits: Fashion and Identity of Women Religious," *Fashion Theory 2*, no. 2 (1998), 189.

11. McNamara, *Sisters in Arms*, 103.

12. Lawrence Cada, Raymond Fitz, Gertrude Foley, Thomas Giardino, and Caron Lichtenberg, *Shaping the Coming of Age of Religious Life* (New York: The Seabury Press, 1979), 19.

13. Tucker and Liefeld, *Daughters of the Church*, 96.

14. Laura Swan, *The Forgotten Desert Mothers: Sayings, Lives, and Stories of Early Christian Women* (New York/Mahwah, NJ: Paulist Press, 2001), 79.

15. William A. Hinnesbusch, *The History of the Dominican Order: Origins and Growth to 1500*, Vol. I (Staten Island, NY: Alba House, 1966), 412–13.

16. Swan, *Forgotten Desert Mothers*, 23, 72.

17. Tucker and Liefeld, *Daughters of the Church*, 151.

18. Patricia Ranft, *Women and the Religious Life in Premodern Europe* (New York: St. Martin's Press, 1996), xiii.

CHAPTER FOUR: CONFORMITY

1. Giles Constable, *Culture and Spirituality in Medieval Europe* (Aldershot, Hampshire, UK: Variorum, 1996), 800.

2. Ibid., 803.

3. Elizabeth A. Clark, *Jerome, Chrysostom, and Friends: Essays and Translations* (New York and Toronto: The Edwin Mellon Press, 1979), 58.

4. Mayo, *History of Ecclesiastical*, 12.

5. Constable, *Culture and Spirituality*, 813–17.

6. Sullivan, "Breaking Habits," 115–16.

7. *Handmaids of the Lord: Contemporary Descriptions of Feminine Asceticism in the First Six Christian Centuries*, selected and translated by Joan M. Petersen (Kalamazoo, MI: Cistercian Publications, Inc., 1996), 75.

8. Clark, *Jerome*, 58, 239.

9. Koslin, "The Dress of Monastic," 55.

10. Elizabeth A. Clark, *Women in the Early Church*, edited by Thomas Halton (Wilmington, DE: Michale Glazier, Inc., 1983), 140.

11. Koslin, "The Dress of Monastic," 57–72.

12. Ranft, *Women and the Religious*, 21.

13. Boulding, "Background to a Theology," 27.

14. Mayo, *History of Ecclesiastical*, 34.

15. Barbara F. Harvey, *Monastic Dress in the Middle Ages* (Oxford: Trustees of the William Urry Memorial Fund, 1988), 9–27.

16. Tucker and Liefeld, *Daughters of the Church*, 144.

17. Koslin, "The Dress of Monastic," 59.

18. McNamara, *Sisters in Arms*, 97.

19. Ranft, *Women and the Religious*, 24.

20. Koslin, "The Dress of Monastic," 103.

21. Ranft, *Women and the Religious*, 37.

22. Sullivan, "Breaking Habits," 117.

23. Koslin, "The Dress of Monastic," 243–54.

24. Harvey, *Monastic Dress*, 8.

25. McNamara, *Sisters in Arms*, 291.

26. Koslin, "The Dress of Monastic," 80.

27. Valerie R. Hotchkiss, *Clothes Make the Man: Female Cross Dressing in Medieval Europe* (New York and London: Garland Publishing, Inc., 1996), 17–19.

28. Ibid., 15–19. Information about Anastasia the Patrician from Swan, *The Forgotten Desert Mothers*, 73; information about Castissima from Abbott, *History of Celibacy*, 78–80.

29. Information in this section is drawn from Marilyn J. Horn, *The Second Skin: An Interdisciplinary Study of Clothing* (Boston: Houghton Mifflin Company, 1968), 110; Phyllis Tortora and Keith Bubank, *A Survey of Costume History* (New York: Fairchild Publications, 1989), 91; and McNamara, *Sisters in Arms*, 372–73.

CHAPTER FIVE: EMBLEM

1. Sources for the section on military and hospital orders include: Francoise Velde, "Women Knights in the Middle Ages" [online]. Available on the World Wide Web: *http://www.heraldica.org/topics/orders/wom-kn.htm*

(December 2001); Ranft, Women and the Religious, 57; Sisters of the Most Holy Trinity, Euclid, OH; McNamara, Sisters in Arms, 257; and Koslin, "The Dress of Monastic," 104–109, 122.

2. McNamara, Sisters in Arms, 359. Additional information in this section is drawn from Eileen Power, Medieval Women (New York and Cambridge: Cambridge University Press, 1975), 98.

3. William Jud Weiksnar, "Force of Habit," *Review for Religious* 55, no. 4 (July–August 1996), 428.

4. Bernstein, *The Nuns*, 37.

5. Dominican Nuns, Monastery of Our Lady of the Rosary, Summit, NJ.

6. Cordelia Warr, "The Striped Mantle of the Poor Clares: Image and Text in Italy in the Latter Middle Ages," *Arte Christiana: An International Review of Art History and Liturgical Arts* 136 (Nov.–Dec. 1998), 418.

7. Tucker and Liefeld, *Daughters of the Church*, 147.

8. Koslin, "The Dress of Monastic," 125.

9. Laura F. Hodges, "A Reconsideration of the Monk's Costume," *Chaucer Review* 26, no. 2 (1991), 143.

10. McNamara, *Sisters in Arms*, 280–81.

CHAPTER SIX: CHARITY

1. Bernstein, *The Nuns*, 144.

2. McNamara, *Sisters in Arms*, 462.

3. Patricia Wittberg, *The Rise and Fall of Catholic Religious Orders: A Social Movement Perspective* (Albany: State University of New York Press, 1994), 81.

4. Ranft, *Women and the Religious*, 117.

5. Daughters of Charity of St. Vincent de Paul, West Central Province Archives, St. Louis, MO; de Gaul quote from Carmel McEnroy, *Guests in Their Own House: The Women of Vatican II* (New York: The Crossroad Publishing Company, 1996), 166.

6. Alex Wengraf, "The Escudo de Monja or Nun's Badge" [online]. Available on the World Wide Web: *http://www.wengraf.com/ecud11.htm* (2002).

7. Kathryn Burns, *Colonial Habits: Convents and the Spiritual Economy of Cuzco, Peru* (Durham and London: Duke University Press, 1999), 119–27.

8. George C. Stewart, *Marvels of Charity: History of American Sisters and Nuns* (Huntington, NY: Our Sunday Visitor Press, 1994), 150–51.

9. McNamara, *Sisters in Arms*, 503, 538.

10. Penny Storm, *Functions of Dress: Tool of Culture and the Individual* (Englewood Cliffs, NJ: Prentice-Hall, 1987), 221; McNamara, *Sisters in Arms*, 558.

11. Sisters of the Presentation, Watervliet, NY.

12. McNamara, *Sisters in Arms*, 556.

13. Ibid., 562.

14. Daughters of Charity of St. Vincent de Paul, West Central Province Archives, St. Louis, MO.

CHAPTER SEVEN: COURAGE

1. Ann Ball, *Modern Saints and Their Faces—Book Two* (Rockford, IL: Tan Books & Publishers, 1991), 189.

2. Bernstein, *The Nuns*, 262.

3. Wittberg, *Rise and Fall*, 81.

4. "I Know Nothing!: Anti-Catholicism and the Know-Nothings" [online]. Available on the World Wide Web at: *http://www.aquinas-multimedia.com/stjoseph/knownothings.htm* (2002).

5. Ball, *Modern Saints*, 190.

6. Christine D. Morkovsky, "The Challenge of Evangelization in Texas: Women Religious and Their Responses," Texas Catholic Historical Society, 1999 [online]. Available on the World Wide Web at: *http://www.history.swt.edu/CSW/volume4/v4morkovsky.htm* (December 2002).

7. Carol K. Coburn and Martha Smith, *Spirited Lives: How Nuns Shaped Catholic Culture and American Life, 1836–1920* (Chapel Hill and London: University of North Carolina Press, 1999), 43.

8. "What Civil War Nurses Wore" [online]. Available on the World Wide Web at: *http://www.edinborough.com/Life/Nurses/Dix.html* (2001).

9. Stewart, *Marvels of Charity*, 185–221.

10. "Sisters of Mercy, Pittsburgh, Pennsylvania" [online]. Available on the World Wide Web at: *http://chausa.org/SPONSOR/CALL0929.ASP*.

11. Sisters of Bon Secours USA, Mariottsville, MD.

12. Sisters of the Holy Cross, Notre Dame, IN, and Hawthorne Dominicans, Hawthorne, NY.

13. Sisters of Francis of Syracuse, NY.

14. McNamara, *Sisters in Arms*, 596.

15. "Biography of Mother Mary Elizabeth Lange, O.S.P." [online]. Available on the World Wide Web: *http://www.louisdiggs.com/obleates/biography.htm* (December 2002).

16. Coburn, *Spirited Lives*, 133–34.

17. Sisters of Providence, Seattle, WA.

18. See Valerie Steel, *The Corset: A Cultural History* (New Haven, CT: Yale University Press, 2001).

19. Wittberg, *Rise and Fall*, 157.

20. Bernstein, *The Nuns*, 260.

21. Suzanne Cita-Malard, *Religious Orders of Women* (New York: Hawthorn Publishers, 1964), 59.

22. McNamara, *Sisters in Arms*, 611.

23. Cita-Malard, *Religious Orders*, 57.

24. Missionaries of Charity, Calcutta, India.

25. Mary Lou Rosencranz, *Clothing Concepts* (New York: The Macmillan Company, 1972), 107; Ann Plosgerth, "The Modernization of the Roman Catholic Sisters' Habit in the United States in the 1950s and 1960s," *Dress* I (1975), 17.

26. "Holocaust Heroes" [online]. Available on the World Wide Web at: *http://www.holocaust-heroes.com/convents.html* (2002).

27. Helenita Colbert, *To Love Me in Truth: Mother Maria Louisa Josefa of the Blessed Sacrament, Servant of God, 1866–1937* (Los Angeles: Carmelite Sisters of the Most Sacred Heart of Los Angeles, 1987), 26–33.

28. Congregation of the Daughters of St. Francis of Assisi American Province, Lacon, IL.

CHAPTER EIGHT: EXPLOSION

1. Plosgerth, "The Modernization," 17.

2. "Modernizing Nun Habits," *Life* 33, no. 24 (December 15, 1952), 16–17.

3. Plosgerth, "The Modernization," 8.

4. Ibid.

5. McEnroy, *Guests*, 109.

6. Plosgerth, "The Modernization," 9–10.

7. Harrison, *Changing Habits*, 107.

8. Plosgerth, "The Modernization," 11.

9. Ibid.

10. Maryknoll Mission, Maryknoll, NY.

11. Monastery of St. Gertrude, Cottonwood, ID.

12. Sullivan, "Breaking Habits," 124–26.

13. Michelman, "Breaking Habits," 176–87.

14. Congregation of Sisters, Servants of the Immaculate Heart of Mary, Scranton, PA.

15. Bernstein, *The Nuns*, 269.

16. Harris, *The Sisters*, 176.

17. Daniel J. Baer and Victor F. Mosele, "Political and Religious Beliefs of Catholic Attitudes Toward Lay Dress of Sisters," *Journal of Psychology* 74 (1970), 77–83.

18. Harris, *The Sisters*, 28–29.

19. McEnroy, *Guests*, 192.

20. Bernstein, *The Nuns*, 151–52.

21. Helen Rose Fuchs Ebaugh, Out of the Cloister (Austin: University of Texas Press, 1977), 141.

22. Harrison, *Changing Habits*, 200.

23. Rosencranz, *Clothing Concepts*, 263.

24. Sandra M. Schneiders, *The New Wineskins: Re-Imagining Religious Life Today* (New York and Mahway, NJ: Paulist Press, 1986), 26.

25. Bernstein, *The Nuns*, 145.

CHAPTER NINE: REMNANTS

1. Center for Applied Research in the Apostolate (CARA), "Frequently Requested Church Statistics" [online]. Available on the World Wide Web at: *http://geargetown.edu/research/cara/bulletin/index.htm* (December 2002).

2. Roger Finke, "An Orderly Return to Tradition: Explaining the Recruitment of Members into Catholic Religious Orders," *Journal for the Scientific Study of Religion* 36, no. 2 (1997), 228; study referenced in text is Rodney Stark and Roger Finke, "Catholic Religious Vocations: Decline and Revival," *Review of Religious Research* 42, no. 2 (2000), 125–45.

3. Albert DiIanni, "A View of Religious Vocations," *America* (February 28, 1998), 7–12.

4. *CARA Formation Directory for Men and Women Religious 1994–1995.* Edited by Sr. Eleace King, IHM, Ed.D. Center for Applied Research in the Apostolate Washington, DC, 13.

5. Daughters of St. Paul [online]. Available on the World Wide Web at: *http://www.daughtersofstpaul.com/daughters/vocations/meetformation1.html* (December 2002).

6. CARA, 12.

Bibliography

❖

In writing this book, I drew upon several outstanding resources for reference and for a significant amount of information—works strongly recommended to readers interested in further study of women religious and the religious habit. For information on religious clothing, I utilized extensively the publications of Giancarlo Rocca, Desiree Koslin, Marcelle Bernstein, Susan Michelman, Rebecca Sullivan, and Ann Plosgerth. For historical information about women religious, I referred widely to Jo Ann McNamara and Patricia Ranft.

The photographs in the Appendix listing of religious habits have been provided courtesy of Catholic University Press of America, which has recently reprinted Fr. Thomas P. McCarthy's 1963 *Guide to the Catholic Sisterhoods of the United States,* an excellent resource for those interested in United States female religious communities. Many other photographs in this book were borrowed from a magnificent collection featured in *Behold the Women,* edited by Dan Paulos, who graciously granted permission for their reproduction here.

MATERIALS AND LETTERS FROM RELIGIOUS COMMUNITY ARCHIVES

Adorers of the Blood of Christ, Wichita, KS.

Congregation of Sisters, Servants of the Immaculate Heart of Mary, Scranton, PA.

Congregation of the Daughters of St. Francis of Assisi, American Province, Lacon, IL.

Daughters of Charity of St. Vincent de Paul, West Central Province Archives, St. Louis, MO.

Dominican Nuns, Monastery of Our Lady of the Rosary, Summit, NJ.

Dominican Sisters of Edmonds, WA.

Franciscan Sisters of Mary Immaculate, Amarillo, TX.

Hawthorne Dominicans, Hawthorne, NY.

Little Company of Mary, Province of the Holy Spirit, Hurtsville, Australia.

Maryknoll Mission, Maryknoll, NY.

Missionaries of Charity, Calcutta, India.

Monastery of St. Gertrude, Cottonwood, ID.

Sisters of Bon Secours USA, Mariottsville, MD.

Sisters of Providence, Seattle, WA.

Sisters of St. Francis of Philadelphia, PA.

Sisters of St. Francis of Syracuse, NY.

Sisters of the Good Shepherd, Province of Mid-North America, St. Louis, MO.

Sisters of the Holy Cross, Notre Dame, IN.

Sisters of the Most Holy Trinity, Euclid, OH.

Sisters of the Presentation, Watervliet, NY.

Society of Our Mother of Peace, Marionville, MO.

BOOKS

Abbott, Elizabeth. *A History of Celibacy: From Athena to Elizabeth I, Leonardo da Vinci, Florence Nightingale, Gandhi, & Cher.* New York: Scribner, 1999.

Abrahams, Israel. *Jewish Life in the Middle Ages.* New York: Macmillan, 1896.

Ball, Ann. *Modern Saints and Their Faces—Book Two.* Rockford, IL: Tan Books & Publishers, 1991.

Bernstein, Marcelle. *The Nuns.* Philadelphia and New York: J. B. Lippincott, 1976.

The Book of Margery Kempe. Translated and introduced by John Skinner. New York: Image Books/Doubleday, 1998.

Bottomley, Frank. *Attitudes to the Body in Western Christendom.* London: Lepus Books, 1979.

Brother Thomas of Celano. *First Life of St. Francis of Assisi.* Translated by Christopher Stace. London: Society for Promoting Christian Knowledge, 2000.

Burns, Kathryn. *Colonial Habits: Convents and the Spiritual Economy of Cuzco, Peru.* Durham, NC, and London: Duke University Press, 1999.

Cada, Lawrence, Raymond Fitz, Gertrude Foley, Thomas Giardino, and Caron Lichtenberg. *Shaping the Coming Age of Religious Life.* New York: Seabury Press, 1979.

The Canon Law: Letter & Spirit: A Practical Guide to the Code of Canon Law. Collegeville, MN: Liturgical Press, 1995.

CARA Formation Directory for Men and Women Religious 1994–1995. Edited by Sr. Eleace King. Washington, DC: Center for Applied Research in the Apostolate, Georgetown University.

Carey, Ann. *Sisters in Crisis: The Tragic Unraveling of Women's Religious Communities.* Huntington, IN: Our Sunday Visitor, Publishing Division, 1997.

Carroll, William H. *The Guillotine and the Cross.* Front Royal, VA: Christendom Press, 1991.

The Catholic Encyclopedia. New York: Robert Appleton Company, 1999.

Cita-Malard, Suzanne. *Religious Orders of Women.* New York: Hawthorn Publishers, 1964.

Clark, Elizabeth A. *Jerome, Chrysostom, and Friends: Essays and Translations.* New York and Toronto: Edwin Mellen Press, 1979.

———. *Women in the Early Church.* Edited by Thomas Halton. Wilmington, Del.: Michael Glazier, Inc., 1983.

Coburn, Carol K., and Martha Smith. *Spirited Lives: How Nuns Shaped Catholic Culture and American Life, 1836–1920.* Chapel Hill and London: University of North Carolina Press, 1999.

Colbert, Helenita. *Mother Maria Louisa Josefa of the Blessed Sacrament, Servant of God, 1866–1937.* Los Angeles: Carmelite Sisters of the Most Sacred Heart of Los Angeles, 1987.

Comby, Jean. *How to Read Church History, Volume 1: From the Beginnings to the Fifteenth Century.* New York: Crossroad Publishing Company, 1985.

Constable, Giles. *Culture and Spirituality in Medieval Europe.* Aldershot, Hampshire, UK: Variorum, 1996.

Costumes of Religious Orders of the Middle Ages. West Orange, NJ: Albert Saiter Publisher, 1983.

Cruz, Joan. *Incorruptibles.* Rockford, IL: Tan Books & Publishers, 1991.

Currier, Charles Warren. *History of Religious Orders: A Compendious and Popular Sketch of the Rise and Progress of the Principal Monastic, Canonical, Military, Mendicant, and Clerical Orders and Congregations of the Eastern and Western Churches, Together with a Brief History of the Catholic Church in Relation to Religious Orders.* New York: Murphy and McCarthy, 1894.

Daly, Mary. *The Church and the Second Sex.* New York: Harper & Row, 1968.

Davenport, Millia. *The Book of Costume, Volume 1.* New York: Crown, 1948.

Dehey, Elinor Tong. *Religious Orders of Women in the United States (Catholic): Accounts of Their Origin, Works and Most Important Institutions.* Hammond, IN: W. B. Conkey Company, 1930.

De Ray, Maria, and George Barres. *Bernie Becomes a Nun.* New York: Farrar, Straus & Cudahy, 1956.

De Vogüé, Albert. *The Rule of Saint Benedict: A Doctrinal and Spiritual Commentary.* Kalamazoo, MI: Cistercian Publications, 1983.

Durant, Will. *The Age of Faith: A History of Medieval Civilization—Christian, Islamic, and Judaic—from Constantine to Dante: A.D. 325–1300 (The Story of Civilization, Volume 4).* New York: Fine Communications, 1997.

Ebaugh, Helen Rose Fuchs. *Women in the Vanishing Cloister: Organizational Decline in Catholic Religious Orders in the United States.* New Brunswick, NJ: Rutgers University Press, 1993.

Eichenstein, Linda. *Women Under Monasticism.* New York: Russell & Russell, 1963.

Elm, Susanna. *"Virgins of God": The Making of Asceticism in Late Antiquity.* Oxford: Clarendon Press, 1994.

Emerging Religious Communities in the United States. Washington, DC: Georgetown University Center for Applied Research in the Apostolate, 1999.

Ewing, Elizabeth. *Everyday Dress, 1650–1900.* London: B. T. Batsford, 1984.

Fiorenza, Elizabeth Schüssler. *In Memory of Her: A Feminist Theological Reconstruction of Christian Origins.* New York: Crossroad Publishing Company, 1983.

Flannery, Austin, ed. *O. P. Vatican Council II: The Conciliar and Post Conciliar Documents.* Northport, NY: Costello Publishing Company, 1992.

Friedan, Betty. *The Feminine Mystique.* New York: Norton, 1963.

Friedman, Philip. *Their Brothers' Keepers.* New York: Holocaust Library, 1978.

Gregory, Brad S. *Salvation at Stake: Christian Martyrdom in Early Modern Europe.* Cambridge, MA: Harvard University University Press, 1999.

Handmaids of the Lord: Contemporary Descriptions of Feminine Asceticism in the First Six Christian Centuries. Selected and translated by Joan M. Petersen. Kalamazoo, MI: Cistercian Publications, 1996.

Harris, Sara. *The Sisters: The Changing World of the American Nun.* Indianapolis and New York: Bobbs-Merrill, 1970.

Harrison, V. V. *Changing Habits: A Memoir of the Society of the Sacred Heart.* New York: Doubleday, 1988.

Harvey, Barbara F. *Monastic Dress in the Middle Ages.* Oxford: Trustees of the William Urry Memorial Fund, 1988.

Heine, Susanne. *Women and Early Christianity: A Reappraisal.* Minneapolis, MN: Augsburg Publishing House, 1987.

Hinnesbusch, William A. *The History of the Dominican Order, Volume 1: Origins and Growth to 1500.* Staten Island, NY: Alba House, 1966.

Hochstettler, Donald. *A Conflict of Traditions: Women in Religion in the Early Middle Ages 500–840.* Lanham, MD: University Press of America, 1992.

The Holy Bible, Douay Reims Version. Rockford, IL: Tan Books & Publishers, 1989.

Horn, Marilyn J. *The Second Skin: An Interdisciplinary Study of Clothing.* Boston: Houghton Mifflin, 1968.

Hotchkiss, Valerie R. *Clothes Make the Man: Female Cross Dressing in Medieval Europe.* New York and London: Garland Publishing, 1996.

John Cassian: The Institutes. Translated and annotated by Boniface Ramsey. New York and Mahwah, NJ: Newman Press, 2000.

Joseph, M. *Out of Many Hearts: Mother Alphonsa Lathrop and Her Work.* Hawthorne, NY: The Servants of Relief for Incurable Cancer, 1965.

Kaiser, Susan B. *The Social Psychology of Clothing: Symbolic Appearances in Context.* New York: Macmillan, 1990.

Kelly, Francis M., and Randolph Schwabe. *A Short History of Costume and Armour.* New York: Scribner & Sons, 1931.

Koslin, Desiree G. "The Dress of Monastic and Religious Women as Seen in Art from the Early Middle Ages to the Reformation." Ph.D. diss., New York University, 1999.

Kraemer, Ross Shepard. *Her Share of the Blessing: Women's Religion Among Pagans, Jews, and Christians in the Greco-Roman World.* New York: Oxford University Press, 1992.

LaPorte, Jean. *The Role of Women in Early Christianity.* New York: Edwin Mellen Press, 1982.

Laver, James. *Costume and Fashion: A Concise History.* New York: Thames & Hudson, 1985.

The Lives of the Desert Fathers [Historia Monachorum in Aegypto]. Translated by Norman Russell. Kalamazoo, MI: Cistercian Publications, 1981.

Mayo, Janet. *A History of Ecclesiastical Dress.* New York: Holmes & Meier Publishers, 1984.

McCarthy, Thomas P. *Guide to the Catholic Sisterhoods of the United States.* Washington, DC: Catholic University Press, 1963.

McEnroy, Carmel. *Guests in Their Own House: The Women of Vatican II.* New York: Crossroad Publishing Company, 1996.

McNamara, Jo Ann. *A New Song: Celibate Women in the First Three Christian Centuries.* Binghamton, NY: Harrington Park Press, 1985.

McNamara, Jo Ann, John E. Halborg, and E. Gordon Whatley. *St.*

Radegund from Sainted Women of the Dark Ages. Durham, NC, and London: Duke University Press, 1992.

————. *Sisters in Arms: Catholic Nuns Through Two Millennia*. Cambridge, MA.: Harvard University Press, 1996.

Moss-Bruce, C. *Of Cell and Cloister: Catholic Religious Orders Through the Ages*. Milwaukee, WI: Bruce Pub. Co., 1957.

Neal, Marie Augusta. *From Nuns to Sisters: An Expanding Vocation*. Mystic, CT: Twenty-Third Publications, 1990.

New Commentary on the Code of Canon Law. Edited by John P. Beal, James A. Coriden, and Thomas J. Green. New York: Paulist Press, 2000.

Nygren, David J., and Miriam D. Ukeritis. *The Future of Religious Orders in the United States: Transformation and Commitment*. Westport, CT, and London: Praeger, 1993.

O'Connor, James I. *The Canon Law Digest, Volume VIII*. Mundelei, IL: Canon Law Digest, 1978.

Off with Her Head: The Denial of Women's Identity in Myth, Religion, and Culture. Edited by Howard Erlberg Swartz and Wendy Donigh. Berkeley, CA: University of California Press, 1985.

Pachomian Koinonia, Volume I: The Life of St. Pachomius and His Disciples. Translated by Armand Veilleux. Kalamazoo, MI: Cistercian Publications, 1980.

Paulos, Daniel. *Behold the Women* Albuquerque, NM: St. Bernadette Institute of Sacred Art, 1997.

Peifer, Claude J. *Monastic Spirituality*. New York: Sheed and Ward, 1966.

Pioneer Healers: The History of Women Religious in American Health Care. Edited by Ursula Stepsis and Dolores Liptak. New York: Crossroad Publishing Company, 1989.

Pomeroy, Sarah B. *Goddesses, Whores, Wives and Slaves: Women in Classic Antiquity*. New York: Shocken Books, 1975.

Power, Eileen. *Medieval Women*. New York: Cambridge University Press, 1975.

Rapley, Elizabeth. *The* Dévotes: *Women and Church in Seventeenth-Century France*. Montreal: McGill-Queen's University Press, 1990.

Ranft, Patricia. *Women and Spiritual Equality in Christian Tradition.* New York: St. Martin's Press, 1998.

————. *Women and the Religious Life in Premodern Europe.* New York: St. Martin's Press, 1996.

RB 1980: The Rule of St. Benedict in Latin and English with Notes. Edited by Timothy Fry. Collegeville, MN: Liturgical Press, 1981.

Rocca, Giancarlo. *La Sostanza dell'Effemero: Gli Abiti egli Ordini Religiosi in Occidente.* Milan: Edizioni Paoline, 2000.

Rogers, Carole Garibaldi. *Poverty, Chastity and Change: Lives of Contemporary Nuns.* New York: Twayne Publishers, 1996.

Rosencranz, Mary Lou. *Clothing Concepts.* New York: Macmillan, 1972.

Ross, Heather Coyler. *The Art of the Arabian Costume: A Saudian Arabian Profile.* Studio City, CA: Empire Publishing Service/Players Press, 1994.

Rubens, Alfred. *A History of Jewish Costume.* New York: Crown, 1973.

Sayers, Dorothy L. *Are Women Human?* Grand Rapids, MI: William B. Eerdmans Publishing, 1971.

Schneiders, Sandra M. *Beyond Patching: Faith and Feminism in the Catholic Church.* New York and Mahwah, NJ: Paulist Press, 1991.

————. *The New Wineskins: Re-Imagining Religious Life Today.* New York and Mahwah, NJ: Paulist Press, 1986.

Stark, Rodney. *The Rise of Christianity: A Sociologist Reconsiders History.* Princeton, NJ: Princeton University Press, 1996.

Steele, Valerie. *Corset: A Cultural History.* New Haven, CT: Yale University Press, 2001.

Steichen, Donna. *Ungodly Rage: The Hidden Face of Catholic Feminism.* San Francisco: Ignatius Press, 1992.

Stewart, George C., Jr. *Marvels of Charity: History of American Sisters and Nuns.* Huntington, IN: Our Sunday Visitor, Publishing Division, 1994.

Storm, Penny. *Functions of Dress: Tool of Culture and the Individual.* Englewood Cliffs, NJ: Prentice-Hall, 1987.

Suenens, Léon Joseph. *The Nun in the World: New Dimensions in the Modern Apostolate.* Westminster, MD: Newman Press, 1962.

Swan, Laura. *The Forgotten Desert Mothers: Sayings, Lives, and Stories of Early Christian Women.* New York and Mahwah, NJ: Paulist Press, 2001.

Tolkien, J. R. R., ed. *Ancrene Wisse: The English Text of the Ancrene Riwle.* London and New York: Oxford University Press, 1962.

Tortora, Phyllis, and Keith Bubank. *A Survey of Costume History.* New York: Fairchild Publications, 1989.

Tucker, Ruth A., and Walter L. Liefeld. *Daughters of the Church: Women and Ministry from New Testament Times to the Present.* Grand Rapids, MI: Academie Books, 1987.

Tugwell, Simon, ed. *Early Dominicans: Selected Writings.* New York: Paulist Press, 1982.

Vision 2002 Religious Vocation Discernment Guide. Chicago: Claretian Publications, 2002.

Weaver, Mary Jo. *New Catholic Women: A Contemporary Challenge to Traditional Religious Authority.* San Francisco: Harper & Row, 1985.

Whelan, Basil. *Historic English Convents of Today: The Story of the English Cloisters in France and Flanders in Penal Times.* London: Burns, Oates & Washbourne, 1936.

Wittberg, Patricia. *The Rise and Fall of Catholic Religious Orders: A Social Movement Perspective.* Albany: State University of New York Press, 1994.

JOURNAL ARTICLES, NEWSPAPER ARTICLES,
AND OTHER MATERIALS

Allen, Marcia. "We Each Take Our Turn: Toward a New Corporate Identity." *LCWR Occasional Papers* (Fall 1996): 11–18.

Baer, Daniel J., and Victor F. Mosele. "Political and Religious Beliefs of Catholics and Attitudes Toward Lay Dress of Sisters." *Journal of Psychology* 74 (1970): 77–83.

Boulding, Sister Maria. "Background to a Theology of the Monastic Habit." *Downside Review* 98, no. 331 (April 1980): 110–23.

Brock, Sebastian. "The Robe of Glory: A Biblical Image in the Syriac Tradition." *The Way* (July 1999): 247–59.

Cox, Betsy. *A Call to Care: Stories of Courage, Compassion and America's Health.*

St. Louis, MO: Catholic Health Association of the United States, 1996. Videocassette (57 minutes).

DiIanni, Albert. "A View of Religious Vocations." *America* (February 28, 1998): 7–12.

Finke, Roger, and Rodney Stark. "Catholic Religious Vocations: Decline and Revival." *Review of Religious Research* 42, no. 2 (December 2000): 125–45.

Gordon, Mary. "Women of God." *Atlantic Monthly* (January 2002): 57–88.

Harmer, Catherine M. "Religious of the Future: A Question of Identity and Image." *LCWR Occasional Papers* (Fall 1996): 19–23.

Hodges, Laura F. "A Reconsideration of the Monk's Costume" *Chaucer Review* 26, no. 2 (1991): 133–46.

Jones, Arthur. "Nuns Renew Vows." *National Catholic Reporter* 35, no. 18 (March 5, 1999): 11–15.

Joseph, Nathan, and Nicholas Alex. "The Uniform: A Sociological Perspective." *American Journal of Sociology* 77, no. 4 (1972): 719–30.

Long, Thomas J. "Influence of Uniform and Religious Status on Interviewees." *American Psychological Journal* (1978): 405–9.

Louis, Meera. "Modern Marketing Helps Sell Life as a Nun." *Wall Street Journal* (May 11, 1999).

Malina, Bruce J., and Jerome H. Neyrey. "Honor and Shame in Luke-Acts," in *The Social World of Luke-Acts: Models for Interpretation*. Edited by Jerome H. Neyrey. Peabody, MA: Hendrickson Publishers, 1991.

Matthews, Jessica. "An Army of Brides." Unpublished conference paper. Popular Cultural Association Meeting, Albuquerque, NM, February 27, 1999.

McCarty, Marty. "Ever Wonder What Nuns Wear to Work?" *Kansas City Star* (December 4, 1999).

McDonough, Elizabeth. "Habit and Habitus: A Brief History." *Review for Religious* (September–October 1997): 547–52.

———. "Habit and Habitus: Current Legislation." *Review for Religious* (November–December 1997): 649–54.

Melamed, Audrey R., Manuel S. Silverman, and Gloria J. Lewis. "Personal

Orientation Inventory: Three-Year Follow-Up of Women Religious." *Review for Religious* 16, no. 2 (Winter 1975): 105–10.

Michelman, Susan. "Breaking Habits: Fashion and Identity of Women Religious." *Fashion Theory* 2, no. 2 (1998): 165–92.

Miller, Mary Claudelle, and Mary Ellen Roach. "Religious Garb: Significant or Sentimental." *Journal of Home Economics* 58, no. 9 (November 1966): 731–34.

Murphy, Elizabeth Ann. "Where Do Mass Media Images of Priesthood and Religious Life Come From?" *Horizon* (Spring 1995): 3–9.

Murphy, Sister Elizabeth Ann. "Sisters and Cigarettes: Icons of Popular Culture." *LCWR Occasional Papers* (Summer 2000): 3–11.

Plogsterth, Ann. "The Modernization of Roman Catholic Sisters' Habits in the United States in the 1950s and 1960s." *Dress: Costume Society of America* 1 (1975): 7–13.

Reardon, Patricia T. "Society's Outdated Image of Religious Women Is a Constant Frustration to Modern Nuns." *Chicago Tribune* (November 21, 1998).

Sullivan, Rebecca. "Breaking Habits: Gender, Class and the Sacred in the Dress of Women Religious," in *Consuming Fashion: Adorning the Transnational Body.* Edited by Anne Brydon and Sandra Neissen. Oxford and New York: Berg, 1998: 109–27.

Swarbrick, Judith. Unpublished original research. Preston, England, 2002.

Tamayo, Juan O. "A Most Merciful Mission: Nuns Help Dominican Prostitutes Battle AIDS." *Miami Herald* (June 23, 1997).

Thompson, Margaret Susan. "Sisterhood and Power: Class, Culture, and Ethnicity in the American Convent." *Colby Library Quarterly* (September 25, 1989): 149–75.

Warr, Cordelia. "Religious Dress in Italy in the Late Middle Ages," in *Defining Dress: Dress as Object, Meaning and Identity.* Edited by Amy de la Haye and Elizabeth Wilson. Manchester and New York: Manchester University Press, 1999: 79–91.

———. "The Striped Mantle of the Poor Clares: Image and Text in Italy in the Latter Middle Ages." *Arte Christiana: An International Review of Art History and Liturgical Arts* 136 (November–December 1998): 415–30.

Weiksnar, William Jud. "Force of Habit." *Review for Religious* 55, no. 4. (July–August 1996): 425–30.

Wittberg, Patricia. " 'Real' Religious Communities: A Study of Authentication in New Roman Catholic Religious Orders." *Religion of the Social Order* 6 (1996): 149–74.

———. "Declining Institutional Sponsorship and Religious Orders: A Study of Reverse Impacts." *Sociology of Religion* 61, no. 3 (Fall 2000): 315–25.

WEBSITE RESOURCES

Agius, Denis. "Benedictines Under Terror 1794–95." English Benedictine Congregation History Commission Symposium, 1982 [online]. Available on World Wide Web: *http://www.catholic-history.org.uk/ebc/1982 agius.pdf.*

"A Journey of Love: Towards a Greater Challenge" [online]. Available on the World Wide Web: *http://www.stmarysmaine.com/sitewide_content/ About_SOCHS/Saint_Marguerite/Great er_Challenge.htm* (December 2002).

"Archive of the Catholic League's Annual Reports on Anti-Catholicism" [online]. Available on the World Wide Web: *http://catholicleague.org/ archive_of_annualreports.htm* (1994–2001).

"Biography of Mother Mary Elizabeth Lange, O.S.P." [online]. Available on World Wide Web: *http://www.louisdiggs.com/oblates/Biography.htm.*

Center for Applied Research in the Apostolate (CARA). "Frequently Requested Church Statistics" [online]. Available on the World Wide Web: *http://www.georgetown.edu/research/cara/bulletin/index.htm* (December 2002).

Congregation of the Sisters, Servants of the Immaculate Heart of Mary [online]. Available on the World Wide Web: *http://ihm.marywood.edu* (December 2002).

"Convents, Church Institutions Sheltered Thousands of Refugees" [online]. Available on World Wide Web: *http://www.holocaust-heroes.com/ convents.html* (1998).

Drake, Barbara H., and Randall E. James, "Extension in Religious Communities." *Journal of Extension* 31, No. 1 (Spring 1993) [online]. Available on World Wide Web: *http://www.joe.org/joe/1993spring/a6.html* (December 2002).

"The Fathers of the Church" [online]. Formatted by the Christian Classics Ethereal Library. Electronic version New Advent, Inc., 1996. Available on the World Wide Web: *http://www.newadvent.org/fathers* (2002).

Hitchcock, James. "Was Vatican II 'Pre-conciliar'?" [online]. *Catholic Dossier Issues Around the World* 6, No. 6 (November/December 2000). Available on the World Wide Web: *http://www.catholic.net/rcc/Periodicals/Dossier/2000-12/column3.html* (December 2002).

Hyatt, Jennifer. "Jesus works in mysterious ways!" [online]. Available on the World Wide Web: *http://www.daughtersofstpaul.com/daughters/vocations/meetformation1.html* (1999).

"I Know Nothing! Anti-Catholicism and the Know-Nothings" [online]. Available on the World Wide Web: *http://www.aquinas-multimedia.com/stjoseph/knownothings.html* (1998).

Levick, Ben. "Christian Clothing: Women's Clothing" [online]. Available on World Wide Web: http://www.angelcynn.ork.uk (2001).

Morkovsky, Christine M. "The Challenge of Catholic Evangelization in Texas: Women Religious and their Response." Texas Catholic Historical Society, 1993 [online]. Available on World Wide Web: *http://www.history.swt.edu/CSW/volume4/v4Morkovsky.htm* (December 2002).

Perry, Mary Catharine. "Lent: Monastery Style." Available on World Wide Web: *http://www.catholicyouth.freeservers.com/vocations/religiouslife/cloister_lent.htm* (December 2002).

"The Singing Nun" [online]. Available on the World Wide Web at: *http://www.swinginchicks.com/singing_nun.htm*, (December 2002).

Stateman, Alison. "Nunsense: Boston Convent Proves PR Isn't Just for the Secular." Public Relations Society of America [online]. Available on the World Wide Web: *http://www.prsa.org/_Publications/magazines/Tactics/0800spot1.html* (December 2002).

Ursuline Sisters of Youngstown. "National Information" [online]. Available on the World Wide Web: *http://www.theursulines.org/national.html* (December 2002).

Velde, François. "Women Knights in the Middle Ages" [online]. Available on World Wide Web: http://www.heraldica.org/topics/orders/wom-kn.htm (December 2001).

Wengraf, Alex. "The Escudo de Monja or Nun's Badge" [online]. Available on World Wide Web: http://*www.wengraf.com/ecud//.htm* 2001.

"What Civil War Nurses Wore" [online]. Available on the World Wide Web: *http://www.edinborough.com/Life/Nurses/Dix.html* (2001).

Index

Page numbers of illustrations appear in italics.